EYES TO SEE UNSEEN ENEMIES

PAUL & LINDA VILLANUEVA

Published by Fifthook Media Digital Publishing

Copyright 2015 Fifthook Media Digital Publishing

No part of this book may be reproduced, copied, stored in a retrieval system, transmitted by any means, electronic, mechanical, photocopying, recording, or otherwise without the express written permission from Fifthook Media Digital Publishing. For other spiritual warfare and Christian living books, please visit our website.

www.fifthookmedia.com

ISBN 978-1-942019-03-9 (Paperback 2nd Ed)

ISBN 978-1-942019-05-3 (eBook 2nd Ed.)

ISBN 978-0-983764-45-8 (eBook 1st Ed.)

Cover photo "Finger Face" by Christopher Bissell at Getty Images licensed for use by Fifthook Media. Rear cover photo "Unseen Enemy" by Paul Villanueva. All Scripture quoted from the King James Version of the Bible.

Table of Contents

PART ONE: THE UNSEEN 4
Introduction 5
Chapter 1: Vision of the Sloth 9
Chapter 2: Spiritual Abandon 22
Chapter 3: Temple of the Sun 31
Chapter 4: Nothing Will Harm You 45
Chapter 5: Living in Covenant 64
PART TWO: IDOLICIDE 76
Killing Idols 77
Chapter 6: Pastor Pride 79
Chapter 7: Desire a Disciple's Heart 85
Chapter 8: Abolish Abominations 88
Chapter 9: Trash Tradition 97
Chapter 10: Flee False Worship 102
Chapter 11: Slaughter Self 108
Chapter 12: Death to Doubt 112
Chapter 13: Rip Apart Religion 117
Chapter 14: Annihilate Addictions 121
Chapter 15: Slay Self Pity 126
Chapter 16: A Unified Christian Language 131
Ministry Information 142
About the Authors 146
Books by the Authors 147

Paul and Linda Villanueva

PART ONE: THE UNSEEN

Introduction

We will be discussing the difference between Biblical Christianity versus Cultural Christianity. Biblical Christianity is that true foundational faith that leads to eternal salvation. Cultural Christianity does not lead to eternal life rather it leads to eternal death. There is no gray or in-between area. Once we understand what Biblical Christianity is, then we can easily recognize what it is not.

It is possible and quite common for people to hear the word of God as contained in the Scriptures, and not obey or do what is commanded in those Scriptures. Many have heard, read, and studied the Bible for numerous years without obeying those words contained in it. The one who obtains eternal salvation and is worthy to eat of the tree of life is the one who not only hears the word, but also obeys the word. They obey **ALL** of God's word. There is no partial salvation and there is no partial obedience.

Our goal is to assist you in gaining eyes to see those unseen enemies that are hidden within the Christian religion, and to expose those demonic forces, which are masquerading in Cultural Christianity. Simultaneously, we desire to steer you into the Biblical truth surrounding real Christian living that leads to overcoming this world of evil. We did not invent this concept; we embraced this idea from the behavior and words of Yeshua of Nazareth contained in the Scriptures. Total obedience to God's word is not our requirement rather it is God's standard for holiness.

In the Gospel of Luke chapter six, Yeshua questions the crowd that had gathered around him, asking them why were they calling him Lord, Lord, and not doing whatever

says? He tells them that every person who comes to him, hears his words, and actually does them is like a wise person who builds their house upon a solid rock foundation. And that is not all. The opposite is true for those who hear his words and do not do them, as their house is built on sandy soil and is soon destroyed when the rains and floods come. This is Biblical Christianity. Cultural Christianity practices the religion but fails to obey the words of God. This book will show you specific ways in which this is done.

In chapter eight of the same Gospel of Luke, Yeshua's mother and family came to talk to him. When he was told they were waiting for him he asked, "Who is my mother and who are my brothers?" He answered his questions by stating that whoever hears the word of God and practices it, those people are his family. There is no gray area, and no partial obedience. Three chapters later, a woman yells to Yeshua, "Blessing to the womb that carried you and to the breasts that suckled you!" A wonderful praise to Maryam, Yeshua's mother, but he responded with, "Blessings to those who have heard the word of God and keep it."

There is just no theological or ideological way around the simple commands to obey all of God's word as outlined for us in the Scriptures. To do otherwise is not Biblical Christianity, but a false anti-Christ religion. We must write and talk about it. The Holy Spirit has shown us visions, dreams, and truths regarding this blindness, and we beg anyone who will listen to repent and turn back to obedience to God's word. **"Son of man, thou dwellest in the midst of a rebellious house, which have eyes to see, and see not; they have ears to hear, and hear not: for they are a rebellious house."** (Ezekiel 12:2).

And Yeshua says, "I know thy works, that thou art neither cold nor hot: I would thou wert cold or hot. So then, because thou art lukewarm, and neither cold nor hot, I will spue thee out of my mouth. Because thou sayest, I am rich, and increased with goods, and have need of nothing; and knowest not that thou art wretched, and miserable, and poor, and blind, and naked. I counsel thee to buy of me gold tried in the fire, that thou mayest be rich; and white raiment, that thou mayest be clothed, and that the shame of thy nakedness do not appear; and anoint **thine eyes** with **eyesalve**, that thou mayest **see**. As many as I love, I rebuke and chasten: be zealous therefore, and repent." (Revelation 3:15-19).

Job 42:5, 6 proclaims, "I have heard of thee by the hearing of the ear: but now mine **eye seeth** thee. Wherefore I abhor myself, and repent in dust and ashes." It was not enough to hear about God. It took Job's faith in God's word for him to see God, thus he obtained eyes to see. Practicing his religion and hearing of God was not equivalent to actually seeing God, which made him see his own need for repentance and for a savior. Likewise, the lukewarm church of Cultural Christianity needs to repent and obtain eyes to see. Our prayer is that this book would be eyesalve and an alarm to a slumbering church before it is too late to repent.

Chapter 1: Vision of the Sloth

In January 2012, my wife Linda and I decided to visit a new church located in a nearby city. On a Sunday morning while Linda was in the shower getting ready to attend the new church, I had already dressed and was putting away my coffee mug when I glanced out of my kitchen window. I saw something, an animal of sorts, moving or dragging itself on my property about 100 feet away from me. This creature startled me because I had lived in the Southern California desert for 13 years, and knew all the different types of animals living there. But what I was seeing was something I never saw before. Both fascinating and frightening, I froze at the window staring at it.

I saw a creature weighing about 30 to 50 pounds, which looked like an ape or a monkey. It was dragging itself along on the dirt using long ape-like frontal arms with its hind legs facing rearward as if they were broke, useless, and dragging. It was slow and meandering along the fence line. It had brown hair with a hump back. It appeared injured, but it was not injured. It moved like it had been hurt, but somehow I knew it was not hurt.

I stared at the thing from my window, and then ran to Linda and yelled, "There is some kind of ape-like creature on our property!" Because she was showering, she could not witness it. I then ran back to another window located in our bedroom, and saw that the strange alien creature was still there on the dirt slowly dragging itself along.

I watched this creature in amazement as it went to a portion of my chain link fence and with one large and long frontal arm, started digging in the dirt. It was slow and methodical. It turned its ape-like face toward me as if to say, "Notice this." I thought to myself, "I have to take a picture of this creature!" I ran to grab a camera, and additionally placed a semi-automatic pistol in my waistband because the animal frightened me, and I was not aware of what it was or what it could do to me. All I knew was that it was the strangest creature I had ever seen. It was creepy.

In a few seconds, I sprinted from the front door to where I had seen the animal. The thing moved so slow that I knew it would still be where I had last seen it. However, when I arrived, it was gone, it had vanished. It was nowhere to be found. I searched the entire area for the creature to no avail. It was not possible for this thing to climb my chain link fence, as it was too slow and cumbersome in movement, and its rear legs were useless. Additionally, I would have seen it on the other side.

I went to the area where it dug in the dirt when it had looked at me as if saying, "Pay attention." I was shocked to find a freshly dug hole by the fence, yet not going underneath the fence. I saw quite a bit of dirt had been recently moved. Now, this was creepy because the animal I was just looking at had vanished, but left "evidence" of its dig for me.

Being very perplexed, we left to attend this new church, but I could not get this creature off my mind all day. I could only think of what I saw. It was so strange and foreign to me. I saw it with my own eyes. I was awake getting ready to leave the house. I was completely in my right mind, so what was it?

We arrived at the church location, and the people were nice but highly charismatic and emotional in their exhibitions so that I felt cautious of possible "kundalini" spirits there. The term kundalini comes from Sanskrit, and literally means snake. In yogic practices, it is the energy that is located at the base of the human spine, and when activated gives mystical experiences. Churches just like any other place where people are gathered in a mystical or spiritual pagan practice can release this kundalini spirit within themselves, and it can become dangerous for others in attendance. We say pagan practices in church, because anytime people worship God in an inappropriate manner, it is idolatry. There is no difference between idol worship to a false god and inappropriate worship to the real God.

During the highly emotionally charged service, people in the congregation began screaming, yelling, and literally running around inside the building. The band was playing loudly with people eagerly getting up from their seats to go pray over others. They would run to someone, place their hands on them, and start praying over them in loud voices. Women were falling on the floor, dancing, or taking laps around the building. It was total chaos.

Several women honed in on Linda. About six females surrounded her, and I could feel them crowding me out and away from my wife. It was as if a predator was thinning the herd by separating the weak from the strong. They started speaking words in her ears, and placing their hands on her while I got pushed back to the rear of Linda. I firmly stood behind her to make sure she did not get pushed backwards in an attempt to get her "slain in the so-called-spirit." I kept praying to God for protection from all "kundalini" or "Christian-witchcraft spirits." I was real cautious and discerning, but was also perplexed as to why I should feel so unsafe in church among other Christians.

There was a deaf and mute man sitting in the front row. During this prayer craze, the man decided to come and pray over me. He started hugging me, and I placed my right hand on his chest with my other hand on his back because I knew he had a deaf and mute spirit in him that needed to come out. I began to pray in the authority of Yeshua against that foul and wicked spirit in him, and began the process of casting it out of him.

Suddenly, he removed my hands from his chest and back, stood in front of me, and held both my hands up toward the ceiling. Then he started "squeaking" like a porpoise or dolphin. This was eerie! Linda heard it also, and felt uncomfortable with what was happening. So, I stopped casting the demon out of him, and just stood there with this man standing in front of me raising both my hands in the air and speaking this squeaking dolphin language over me.

Finally, the service started again, and he left me to go back to his seat. I did not like what had happened and felt weird about the whole thing. Honestly, even though the red flag warnings were screaming in our faces, we both were considering getting involved in this church and becoming a part of them. Yet, I knew something was wrong. Still, throughout the entire remaining service, I thought of that strange alien monkey-faced creature I had seen crawling on my property that morning.

Later in the week, both Linda and I experienced demonic attacks. While conducting some research for our radio program in our office, I heard a buzzing insect-like sound that seemed to be flying around my head, but there was no insect actually present in the room. Suddenly, it felt as if something flew inside of my right ear. Immediately, I heard "feed-back" and a high-pitched sound in my head. I knew it was the spirit of deafness, a demonic entity, and I knew exactly from where it came; it came from the deaf and mute man that placed his hands on me at church! This demon wanted to give me deafness, and it was transferred to me from the man who had the spirit of deafness in him. I began to realize that attending a church operating in kundalini energy was not only a bad idea, but highly dangerous for a Biblical Christian.

Using the authority of Yeshua, which he has given all Biblical followers, I stopped the demon and expelled it away from me. This occurred three separate times, when that foul and wicked spirit attempted to give me disease. Yeshua commanded all true Biblical Christians to cast out or violently expel demonic spirits. The expulsion begins with the individual getting rid of these nasty things. Yeshua declared in Mark 16:17, "And these signs shall follow them that believe; in my name shall they cast out devils." Biblical Christians believe in the total word of God without mental reservation.

Linda also began experiencing demonic problems after the visit to the emotionally extravagant church with their "holiness" dress and charismatic-kundalini antics. The women, who had "prayed" over her, had indeed transferred numerous demonic spirits, which were now attempting to gain a foothold in Linda's life.

First, Linda felt elation, as if the kundalini serpent energy was writhing inside of her, and this was mixed with a heaviness of heart and weeping. She had a desire to dress like the women in "holiness" attire, which is the result of a religious spirit taking hold. She simply did not feel right, and knew in her spirit that something was amiss.

Once we recognized the transference of demons from the church people, we immediately bound, removed, and expelled them from our lives in the authority of Yeshua our savior. We needed to go through several self-deliverance sessions to get all those filthy spirit beings away from us. So much had happened in the last few days, but it all started when I saw a sloth on my property.

During this strange time, my sister had a troubling dream about me. She dreamed of a giant ugly slug chasing her, and she called out to me for help. I was in another room with an evil man that my sister did not like. But, I came out to protect her from this giant ugly slug, and suddenly this ugly slug turned into a cute little puppy dog.

I picked up the dog and it started licking my face. My sister screamed at me saying, "It is not what you think it is. It is a sloth!" However, I would not listen to her. The evil man I was with grinned and said, "Paul, bring it home to Linda. She will love it." The nightmare ended with my sister trying to warn me about this giant ugly slug she called a sloth. She immediately told me about the dream.

Now this is important. My sister in her waking state did not know what the word sloth meant. She told me that the term sloth was clear in her dream and she even knew how to spell it. I related I thought a sloth was some type of animal, and the term "slothful" was used in the Bible for lazy and dumb-witted. But, that was all I knew about it.

Immediately Linda and I start doing some research on this dream because it sounded very legitimate and cautionary. While I was still talking to my sister on the phone about the dream, Linda researched the word sloth using the Internet. What she saw was shocking! She saw pictures of an animal that looked exactly like the description I gave her of the strange vanishing creature I had seen a few weeks earlier!

Understand, that my sister, Linda, nor I were familiar with the sloth animal before this moment. However, Linda knew by the pictures on the computer screen in front of her, a sloth was the animal I had seen on our property. But, here lies the huge problem; sloths live in the tropical rainforests of Central and South America, not in the deserts of Southern California! They cannot survive outside of the rainforest. It would have been impossible for me to see a real sloth on our property.

We then began studying the sloth and its unique behavior in the rainforest. As I watched videos of this animal and viewed pictures of it, I knew without a doubt that it was in fact a sloth that I had seen crawling on the dirt on my property in the Southern California desert just weeks prior. Additionally, we began to study the word "slothful" as it is presented in the Scriptures. It was a fascinating study, and we began to realize some wisdom in all of this.

At this point, I knew that I had seen a vision. It was a waking vision pregnant with meaning and a message. I had peered into another realm, a spiritual dominion, and my eyes had been open to see things not seen with the natural eye. And yes, the sloth has a monkey-like or ape-like appearance.

The sloth lives most of its entire life hanging from a branch in any given tree in the rainforests of Central and South America. Sloths only move when it is necessary, and then very slowly. They have only a quarter of the muscle mass of other animals in their same weight class. They mate and give birth to their young while hanging from a branch, and surprisingly some animals have been found dead while continuing to hang upside down in their tree.

It moves its body so little that its fur hosts a green bacterium, as well as a host of other insects. Also, the green bacteria camouflages and protects them from predators while hanging in the trees. The sloth is a creature of the night. It is nocturnal. It has small ears and large eyes, but does not see or hear well, instead relying on its sense of smell.

Their diet is limited to the leaves and buds of the tree in which they live. They only eat from the tree that they live and die in, and thus their diet consists of nothing more than what can be reached by its slow lazy arms. Their metabolism is so low that they make use of little to no nutrients from their minimal diet by barely moving, and so they expend little to no energy.

If a sloth is on the ground, they cannot move well, and are very slow in pulling their bodies along with their large frontal arms. They drag themselves on the ground and drag their hind legs behind them because the rear legs are useless. On the ground, they are most vulnerable to predators, and so live their entire lives hanging from a tree branch in safety. The sloth only comes down from its tree about once a week to visit the ground to urinate and defecate on it, and then it goes back into the tree to hang on its branch.

An interesting point regarding numbers in the Scriptures can be found in the sloth's neck bones or cervical vertebrae. The majority of mammals have "seven" vertebrae. Seven is God's perfect number, and is contained throughout the Scriptures as a symbol of perfection and completeness.

However, the two-toed sloth has only "six" vertebrae and the three-toed sloth has "nine." Scripturally, the number "six" is the number of man, and it is man who is imperfect, destitute, and void without God. The number "nine" is the last of the single digits and so marks finality and the end. It is also related to "six" in that it is the sum of its factors, thus it means the end of man, and is the number of judgment and finality.

In traditional Christian moral tradition, slothfulness is one of the seven deadly sins. It is defined as spiritual or emotional apathy neglecting what God has spoken. It is the wasting away of gifts God has given a person. It is of course, laziness when it comes to the study and acting out in godly behavior the tenants of Scripture. In other words, it is the lack of true Biblical Christianity. Thomas Aquinas said about slothfulness that it is "sluggishness of the mind which neglects to begin good...It is evil in its effect, if it so oppresses man as to draw him away entirely from good deeds."

Biblically, the term "slothful" is found numerous times referring to a lazy person. Interestingly, the Hebrew words translated slothful also means sluggish or sluggard. Some of the words carry the connotation of deceitfulness with it.

Remember the dream of my sister who saw the giant ugly "slug" that deceitfully turned into a "cute puppy," and finally, was revealed as a "sloth." The Hebrew words mean to lean idly, be indolent, to be slack, false, treacherous, remiss, and deceitful. The spirit behind the word is much more than being lazy, but actually deceitful to the point of treachery. Slothful people are dangerous to others around them.

In the Greek New Testament, Yeshua used a word translated "slothful" in the King James Version of the Bible to describe an irksome, indolent, and sluggish servant (Matthew 25:26). The writer of the book of Hebrews wrote, "That ye be not slothful, but followers of them who through faith and patience inherit the promises" (Hebrews 6:12). The Greek word used means literally to be lazy or figuratively stupid, dull, indolent or slow. However, it is a derivative of a word meaning illegitimate son or a bastard. A bastard is one born not from lawful wedlock. So, the spirit behind the Greek words translated "slothful" mean much more than laziness, they mean illegitimate, not lawful, one that is slow and stupid.

After everything we experienced with the vision, the church, the dream, and the research, we knew we had been beckoned to find the truth from God. As it was prophesied concerning the end of the age in Joel 2:28, "...I will pour out my spirit upon all flesh and your sons and daughters shall prophesy, your old men shall dream dreams, your young men shall see visions."

Also, the Apostle Peter in Acts 2:19 quoting the Prophet Joel said, "And I (God) will shew wonders in the heaven above and signs in the earth beneath." Signs, marks, omens, dreams, visions, and prophetic words from God to reveal truth to the followers of God in the times preceding his final judgment. Certainly seeing a vision of a tropical rainforest sloth in the California desert got our attention.

Linda and I prayed and fasted for an answer from God, and he gave us the insight and interpretation regarding all the "high strangeness" that we had experienced. God revealed to us that the sloth represented the current Cultural Christian church's condition. Moreover, the sloth represented the vast majority of Christian organizations that are called "church."

From the cold, dead, lifeless denominations that have a form of godliness but deny the very power of his spirit, to the hyper-charismatic churches that lack a true Biblical faith; they are all slothful in the eyes of God. Just like the message to the angels overseeing the seven churches in the book of Revelation, God says, "Repent or I'll remove you!" to the majority of those represented.

The Apostle Peter in Acts chapter two knew that it was the last age before the great and terrible day of the Lord, when all the wicked would be destroyed and the righteous in God would be delivered. He knew that from the time of God becoming flesh in his son Yeshua the Messiah and completing his redemptive plan for humans, to the time of the end of the age, was and is the period in which we all live. And it is ending.

For even Peter states in his first epistle, "For the time is come that judgment must begin at the house of God: and if it first begin at us, what shall the end be of them that obey not the gospel of God?" Peter continues, "And if the righteous scarcely be saved, where shall the ungodly and the sinner appear?" (1Peter 4:17, 18). God reveals that the church, the Cultural Christianity that is the majority of Christian religion, shall be judged!

Again, no matter if the church is a cold religious monolith, or a hyper-spirit driven extravagant entertainment piece, or any safe moderate tepid gathering in between, the issue is they are sloth-like. No matter the name or religious ritual, the church is in big trouble and about to be judged. Judgment always begins at the house of the Lord. God called us "out of her" to be among a small number of his people standing on the wall giving warning to anyone who will listen. Revelation 18:4, 5 demands, "...Come out of her, my people, that ye be not partakers of her sins, and that ye receive not of her plagues. For her sins have reached unto heaven and God hath remembered her iniquities."

There is a remnant, a small band of Christians who wish and strive to obey the word of God, and live under his covenant. There is a "remnant resistance" against the failed post-modern-neo-pagan-cultural-church. The fact is that God is calling his army together. We are in a war. We have no time for slothfulness and religious antics. Humans are sick, hurt, and demonized. They need healing, comfort, and spiritual deliverance. They need to be baptized in the real Holy Spirit, displaying the real Biblical gifts of the Spirit. We, the remnant resistance, have to start operating in the fullness of the spiritual gifts again, edifying and building up one another, the true Biblical church.

Chapter 2: Spiritual Abandon

Returning to the description of sloth behavior, we will unpack the same teaching God revealed to us regarding the majority of churches existing today. We say majority because not all churches are slothful or neo-pagan, and if one finds a true Biblical church with Biblical leadership, one must pray, support, and do everything in the power of God to keep it that way. However, just as Yeshua in the book of his Revelation reprimanded six out of seven angelic leaders overseeing the churches because the vast majority were in error in one form or another, he also warns today's churches of impending judgment.

The sloth lives most of its entire life hanging from a branch in any given tree in the rainforests of Central and South America. Sloths only move when it is necessary, and then very slowly. They have only a quarter of the muscle mass of other animals in their same weight class.

Cultural Christians attending tax-exempt business model boxes for feel good entertainment and religious reasons are like the sloth living in their own private tree. Whether or not it is a major denomination, non-denominational, spirit filled or spirit-denied, the church does not want anything to do with other churches or Christians not of their same private tree or religious bias.

Some of the churches that have become a "brand name" seen in every city across America become very cult-like when it comes to outsiders or to those members who leave the tree "brand." The Cultural churches move very slowly when it comes to doing actual Biblical based behaviors, such as repentance from sin, fully trusting in God's word, and casting out demons. Because they prefer to just hang around in their own little tree world, their spiritual muscles have atrophied and have become nearly useless. They are highly religious, but lack true Biblical knowledge and experience.

They mate and give birth to their young while hanging from a branch, and surprisingly some animals have been found dead while continuing to hang upside down in their tree.

Today's churches teach error upon error, and repeat the same heresies or doctrinal lies to every new generation of neo-pagan babies born in their tree. Deep saturated study of the Scriptures is lacking. Instead, on any typical Sunday morning, the congregation is exposed to live entertainment in the guise of worship music, some videos, jokes, announcements, and finally about 30 to 40 minutes of a motivational speech erroneously referred to as a sermon.

The mid-week Bible studies are no better. Here the leader often guides the few in attendance from a book written by one of their favorite "tree" authors, or leads the study from curriculum the pastor has authorized. The deep things of God are simply not searched out.

Due to the lack of Biblical teaching and deliverance from demonic spirits, each generation of spiritual sloths pass on their deception and laziness to the next generation. They prefer to watch entertaining preachers on television and satellite, and just accept whatever they say is true. They prefer to read the latest books in their so called Bible book stores; books full of psychology, new-age thought, and Luciferian doctrine. If it is written by a famous person of the "tree," then it is taken as truth.

The slothful Christian loves conferences and concerts where the famous "tree" teachers teach so they do not have to think for themselves or study Scripture to show themselves approved by God. They are lazy and slothful.

They have turned to delusion, and have died in their tree. They are spiritually dead, hanging onto a branch of deception and lies, empty inside and weak on the outside. Everything that is dead should be buried, but the slothful continue to take up space in their tree of lies, hanging there dead as dead can be.

It moves its body so little that its fur hosts a green bacterium, as well as a host of other insects. Also, the green bacteria camouflages and protects them from predators while hanging in the trees.

The church of the sloth, hanging there in its own tree, barely moving in the things of God, gather unto itself a host of demonic spirits, which gladly live in and among them. Christians full of demons, walking around the church with every imaginable disease and ailment possible, and accepting every doctor's report about them rather than trusting in the word and promises of God. The church of the sloth is embedded with the things of the world. They allow every care and concern of the Luciferian matrix to enter them, believing they can serve and love two masters, God and idolatry.

The demons assist in hiding the slothful Christian from the less discerning. Often, the demons of religion will camouflage the false brethren fooling even the most astute Biblical Christian. The evil spirits of disease, disorder, chaos, mental disturbances, and financial poverty do not want to be exposed to the light. They protect the slothful one from the Biblical Christian who can offer help and deliverance in the authority of Yeshua.

The sloth is a creature of the night. It is nocturnal. It has small ears and large eyes, but does not see or hear well, instead relying on its sense of smell.

Biblical Christians, the true church of Christ, are creatures of the day. The Apostle Paul told the Thessalonians, "Ye are all children of the light, and the children of the day: We are not of the night, or of darkness." (1Thessalonians 5:5). The church of the sloth is a creature of the darkness, having eyes, they do not see well, and having ears, they do not hear well the things of God. Romans 11:8 states, "...God hath given them the spirit of slumber, eyes that they should not see, and ears that they should not hear unto this day."

Their diet is limited to the leaves and buds of the tree in which they live. They only eat from the tree that they live and die in, and thus their diet consists of nothing more than what can be reached by its slow lazy arms. Their metabolism is so low that they make use of little to no nutrients from their minimal diet by barely moving, and so they expend little to no energy.

The church of the sloth limits its spiritual diet to junk food, feasting on cake of the worship music, audio-visual technology, and an entertaining speech. The bulk of its weight sits in its stomach as undigested, rotting, and putrid poison. They only eat what is in reach of their lazy arms. Mystical practices, emergent nonsense, new-age beliefs, satanic business goals, and a diluted gospel fit only for monetary gain and fame. The sloth church looks nothing like the first century church of Yeshua our savior, replacing "social works" for the true ministry of love, repentance, and deliverance.

Hanging from a tree branch, hidden and camouflaged, they dine on their own glorious experiences of mysticism or self-deluded religion of works. Because there are little to no nutrients in their spiritual diet, they starve. It is a slow painful deluded death of demonic deception, torment, and lies. The leaders have convinced the sloths of the deception, "working" in the church equals working for God. They have mistaken the Biblical mandates and work of the Lord for the idolatrous lord of the work. They worship the work as lord rather than recognizing the work as an outflow from the worship of the Lord.

In contrast, Biblical Christians feast on the things of God. It is written in Psalms 78:25, "Man did eat angel's food: he sent them meat to the full." And in Proverbs

30:8, 9, "Remove far from me vanity and lies: Give me neither poverty nor riches; feed me with food convenient (prescribed portion) for me: Lest I be full, and deny thee and say who is the Lord, or lest I be poor, and steal and take the name of my God in vain."

The slothful church is both full and poor. They are full of toxic junk food and deny God, and they are poor and starving, stealing from every non-Biblical source within reach.

On the ground, they are most vulnerable to predators, and so live their entire lives hanging from a tree branch in safety. The sloth only comes down from its tree about once a week to visit the ground to urinate and defecate on it, and then it goes back into the tree to hang on its branch.

Like the sloth, the neo-pagan Christianity of today only "comes down to earth" to pee and poop on it and then it climbs back up to its safety in the tree. They are so religiously minded that they are no earthly good. The hurting and desperate humans need the true church of God to offer God's character and grace to them. Rather, the church of the sloth only uses the people for gain in numbers and in finances.

Sloth Christianity will gladly protest the abortion clinics, urinate and defecate on them, and suddenly disappear up their religious tree to hang around until the next good "work" comes along. Sloths love to point out the sin of homosexuality while secretly cheating on their taxes, or downloading pornography from the Internet. They urinate and defecate on the people and then find repose in their tree of self-righteousness. In contrast, Biblical Christianity recognizes no difference in any given sin. Sin is sin. And all sin must be met with genuine repentance, forgiveness, and salvation.

Did Linda and I fabricate all of this sloth knowledge? As usual, we turn to the Scriptures to verify everything we receive. Now let us examine just a few of the Scriptures about the slothful church.

"Slothfulness casteth into a deep sleep; and an idle soul shall suffer hunger" (Proverbs 19:15). The church, as the sloth, sleeps and suffers spiritual starvation and malnutrition.

"By much slothfulness the building decayeth; and through idleness of the hands the house droppeth through." (Ecclesiastes 10:18). The church has decayed and lost its footing and relevance to the lost and dying world of humans.

"The slothful man saith, there is a lion without, I shall be slain in the street." (Proverbs 22:13). As Satan goes about the people as a roaring lion, seeking to devour them, the slothful church is afraid of spiritual warfare and frightened of the mandate to confront and cast out demons.

"The slothful hideth his hand in his bosom; it grieveth him to bring it again to his mouth." (Proverbs 26:15). Again, the sloth church cannot and will not feed itself on the true Biblical knowledge of God; rather they opt for low-density junk food. It is too much work to diligently study the word of God. It is too much effort to live out its principles.

"The slothful man roasteth not what he took in hunting: but the substance of a diligent man is precious." (Proverbs 12:27). The modern church gathers numbers using modern marketing and business techniques. However, once they attract attendees, they are too slothful to actually disciple and train them in the ways of God. The numbers seldom become Biblical Christians unless God intervenes and drives them out.

"...Be not slothful to go, and to enter to possess the land." (Judges 19:9). Slothful Christianity will not conduct self-deliverance of demons on itself. They refuse to conquer the demons causing sin and disease. They would rather refuse to believe in the mandates of our Lord to do so.

"His lord answered and said unto him, thou wicked and slothful servant, thou knewest that I reap where I sowed not, and gather where I have not strawed." (Matthew 25:26). Yeshua gives this parable to show his extreme dislike for the slothful church that refuses to multiply the gifts the Lord has graciously entrusted.

The above Scriptural references are but a few containing the various Hebrew and Greek words translated as sloth or slothfulness, but the Bible is full of Scripture denouncing paganism and idolatry for God's people. The tale of the slothful church can be boiled down to two anti-commandments: placing other gods alongside, with, or instead of God, and second, the lack of godly care for others. Just as the greatest commandment is to love God with all of our heart, soul, and might (Deuteronomy 6:5) and second, to love others as ourselves (Mark 12:31), the slothful church conducts itself opposite of this mandate. The church of the sloth violates the Ten Commandments, or mandates of God, thus ignoring his never changing, and never ending moral law. Because it places itself over and above the living God, it serves its own interest. Likewise, because it lacks genuine godly character, it treats humans as numbers for financial gain, ignoring the mandate to make disciples of them, and they deceive and steal from their flock.

This would be an excellent time to revisit God's moral law; the ten stipulations to the covenant he makes with us. As we know, living under the covenant brings blessings, and violating the covenant brings curses. However, we will have to wait and revisit them later in this work. First, we wish to unveil another strange vision. This time, the vision occurred during an actual church service.

Chapter 3: Temple of the Sun

Several months after receiving the vision of the slothful church, in March of 2012, Linda and I felt led in our spirits to visit another church on a Sunday morning. The building was located on a neatly manicured property with ample parking that highlighted the largeness of the structure.

An oddly shaped monolith with huge glass panes and sharp geometrical lines gave us the impression that the place was financially secure. It was a huge "campus" with many other smaller buildings hosting numerous activities. Cars and pedestrians filled the asphalt lot while white busses emblazoned with the church's logo spewed forth its cargo of young adults at the front doors.

The odd thing about this particular church structure was its shape. It sat on ample acreage to have been built along traditional lines, but instead seems to have been designed to display a more "artsy" kind of feel. It is obvious even at first glance that this structure was not built with efficiency in mind. One could clearly see that the property could have been utilized much more effectively in supporting the structure.

The front entrance was located in some cock-eyed corner rather than facing the east-west running highway located just yards away. Surrounded by asphalt parking lots, which pushed the church structure toward a narrow slice of land gave it the impression that it was squeezed into the space unnecessarily.

Why is this important? It is relevant because the outside structure gave shape to the interior of the building, and that revelation was a shocker. We will give you eyes to see in a moment.

A few weeks after attending this particular church, I attempted to research the reasons why the building was situated as it was on the land. I spoke with an ex-board member from the church, which was present during the entire building process, and knew just about everything regarding the structure. He said the building was constructed by a local company whose owner was also a member of that church.

The company had hired an outside architect to design the structure. The board members liked the plan and approved it without further questioning. No one really knew why the structure was situated or designed as it was. When I inquired who had overseen the interior decorations and "feel" of the inside, he stated it was the members of the family, which owned the construction company.

There was something wrong with me on that Sunday morning while visiting this church. I had this sick pit in my stomach, the kind of gut gnawing nausea I usually get around demons, or around occult objects infused with magic. Linda is even more sensitive than I am in this area with her stomach pounding out a strong pulsating sickness when she is near anything or anyone that is satanic. It acts like a warning flag, but on this particular Sunday, only I had the gnawing feeling of warning in my gut. Additionally, my lower back was hurting. I could hardly walk, and was feeling somewhat discouraged by what I considered a demonic attack on my body. Linda faithfully prayed for me.

The entire drive to the church was filled with anxiety. Perhaps I was still gun shy from the last episode of demonic church people, or perhaps this was something different. I begged Linda to be extra alert and discerning, and not allow anyone to touch her or pray over her. She assured me that she had her entire armor of God upon her. It is hard to explain, but I felt as if we were entering a danger zone, and we both had to be alert to recognize the deceptions of the evil one.

I felt a weird sort of fear and hyper-spiritual awareness at the same time. I can only describe it like this. It was as if I had been fasting and praying for numerous days with its resulting spiritual sensitivity. But, I had not been fasting. Yet, I had this hyper-spiritual awareness, and I sensed danger!

We walked in past the ushers and smiling people and took a seat in the middle of this large expanse of a building. Still feeling queasy in the stomach, I noticed that I was hyper vigilant in protecting Linda from transference of spirits, the kind that came home with us the last time we visited a pagan worship site disguised as a church of God.

The service started and the band played loud upbeat songs to get the juices flowing. So far so good, I thought. Then about three songs into the service, the tone changed to a shower of ballads. It was then that many people left their seats, walking to the front of the stage that supported the band, and in front of long bench-like altars, began to cry, scream, shake, and place their hands on one another's heads.

I watched in horror as I witnessed once again, the seething serpent energy of kundalini. It was the same kundalini energy that the Hindu yogis activate in their parishioners by stimulating the chakras with the third eye or pineal gland located inside the forehead.

There is a form of new-age eastern mysticism that has invaded the modern church. Believing that they were being touched by the Spirit of God, they traded their discernment for the experiences of being "blessed." Believing that the golden calf was the god who brought them out of Egypt, they rose up and played, sung and danced before it. Believing they were worshipping the true God of creation, they replaced him with the inappropriate worship of eastern religions. And they were fully unaware of these facts.

My lower back was hurting badly, and I had to sit down in the pew while the majority of the people were standing and "worshipping" in pagan rhythms. Linda sat down beside me and told me that God had given her a word for me. She said, "The pain in your back is for a reason and for a season. It is temporary and will leave soon." I accepted that word without fully understanding it.

I placed my arm around Linda and we "hunkered down" in the pew like two soldiers hiding inside a foxhole while bombs and bullets were flying around just above our heads. There, hunkered down in the pew, we were safe from the spirits whizzing above us. We peered out above the bench in front of us and witnessed the serpent energy take over the people. It was like watching an apocalyptic zombie movie.

We saw people undulating and shaking their arms in the space above them while looking around to see who was watching them being "blessed." We saw others stalking the aisles searching for victims to pray with, or to speak a "prophetic word" to. Some were placing their hands on the foreheads of others who unwittingly came to the front altars for prayer, thus getting kundalini spirits transferred to them. We saw women grabbing other's faces and pulling them close so they could impart the "spirit" on them. And we could see the expressions of the victims leaving the altar area after they received prayer, and they did not display the peace of God, rather they looked confused, frightened, and in despair.

I held Linda tight and told her that we needed to appear to be praying privately so that no other person would approach us and attempt to "minister" to us. We could not make eye contact with any of the roving band of spiritual zombies looking for victims to infect with their serpent energies. The experience was frightening!

We were in our little foxhole, dodging demonic bullets while keeping an eye on what was happening around us. It was then I realized that the pain in my back prevented us from standing up and being seen and targeted by these zombies. The pain forced me to sit down, and by sitting down and protecting Linda, we were passed over by those people who were creeping up and down the aisles searching for their next blood sacrifice.

The next day, all the back pain left me. The word of God was true, it was for a reason (protection) and for a season (the time spent in that church), and it was temporary.

Finally, the music stopped, and the people returned to their seats. After a few announcements and generic "prophetic" words spoken to the congregation, the pastor began to give his sermon for the day. Frankly, I do not remember what was said because my eyes begun to be opened to another world around me.

I sat in the pew while the pastor spoke his sermon, and I began to see things around me differently. It was not a vision of things that did not exist, like the vision of the sloth I had earlier, rather it was an understanding about things that existed around me.

First, I noticed the front of the church where the pastor was standing had several steps leading up to the stage. Behind him were huge glass panes facing directly east allowing the morning sun to shine into the expanse. The structure was built so that the glass panes on the east side were in a direct east location to capture the rising sun. In front, flanking both sides of the church stage were tall white Greco-Roman style pillars, and to the rear of the building were two more giant pillars on the north and south sides of the building. The rear of the church was located in the west; this is where the people entered the church.

Each cardinal direction shot past each of the four pillars in sharp triangular geometric patterns, and came to four points inside of the building, so that the points appeared as a triangle over another triangle. Looking from the ceiling, the pattern would be a triangle shape at the front of the sanctuary resting on an upside down or reverse triangle shape at the rear of the sanctuary.

There were two long benches or altars stretching across the front of the steps leading to the stage. Near those altars, during the worship service, the people had gathered around with some kneeling down to pray on them. There we had seen the kundalini spirits manifesting. Two undersized pedestals resembling smaller versions of the Greco-Roman pillars were located at either side of the long altars situated in front of the stage. There were pedestals on the north side and on the south side of the church. On top of each pedestal, a statue of a cherub-type angel with its wings spread out above the altars looked down on the congregants. The heads of the cherubs were decorated with a green leafy wreath, as if care had been taken to "dress" them.

The above description of the interior of the church we had visited, is the interior of a Masonic temple! It is a temple to the sun god, the Blazing Star, the Dog Star, Sirius, or Lucifer. Do we believe the church leadership approved and sanctioned the building to appear like a pagan temple on purpose? We do not know.

We believe that the enemy of our souls is so crafty and deceptive, that unless a Christian has eyes to see their unseen enemies, and exercises their God given discernment in spiritual matters using the Scriptures as a basis for all truth, then they can and will be deluded. The fact remained the interior of the church was set up like a Masonic lodge to worship in the east where the Blazing Star or Lucifer (shiny light one) rises.

How did we know the interior of the church looked like a Masonic temple? We knew because I had been a third degree Master Mason "raised" to the third degree in one of two lodges located in Riverside, California, and Linda had attended many functions with me inside of that lodge. The day we visited the church and God revealed these things to me, I kept them to myself until we arrived home. I then drew out on paper what I had seen inside that church building. When I showed it to Linda, I asked her what it looked like, and she said, "It is a Masonic lodge." Only after her statement did I show her that the drawing was in fact the interior of the church we had just visited!

All Masonic lodges, at least in principle, face east. Even if the actual building does not literally face east, once inside, all members align themselves to the principle that their lodge faces east. Masons enter their lodge from the west. The reason for this is that the "Worshipful Master" sits in the east where the rising sun is located. But it is not really the sun that is important; rather it is the star Sirius, the Dog Star, or Blazing Star. It is Lucifer, the bright one, that is represented by the Worshipful Master seated in the east.

The Worshipful Master is the leader or head of any particular lodge, and often simply is referred to as "Worshipful" most of the time. The east location within a lodge is of most importance. Behind the throne of the Worshipful Master, who represents the Blazing Star in human form, is a representation of the Blazing Star. This lighted five-pointed pentagram is also located on the ceiling of most Masonic lodges.

Every cardinal direction has its function except the north. The north parts of all Masonic lodges are kept in the dark, and no member will ever sit in any seat located in the north. Various reasons are given for this, but it reminds us of the Scripture found in Psalms 48:2, "Beautiful for situation, the joy of the whole earth, is mount Zion, on the sides of the north, the city of the great King."

Perhaps in a Lucifer worshipping pagan temple such as a Masonic lodge, Satan does not want to be reminded of the real and only great King who sits on the sides of the north, and thus wants it dark. Just as it is written about Lucifer in Isaiah 14:13, "For thou hast said in thine heart, I will ascend into heaven, I will exalt my throne above the stars of God: I will sit also upon the mount of the congregation, in the sides of the north." However, in verse 15 Isaiah writes about Lucifer's ambitious plan, "Yet, thou shalt be brought down to hell, to the side of the pit."

In a lodge, there are two important Greco-Roman pillars flanking either side of the room. One is called Jachin and the other Boaz, meaning beauty and strength. Preceding the steps leading to the Worshipful Master seated in the east is an altar. No member is allowed to step between the altar and the worshipful Master. It is on this altar that members take their horrific blood oaths of secrecy. It is on this altar to Lucifer that the member kneels and swears on a holy book depending on that member's religious preferences.

On the sacred book is placed one of Freemason's best-known symbols, a square with a compass. The square on top is an upright triangle, and the compass on the bottom makes an upside down triangle. The two make four distinct geometric points when touching each other. The three items on a Masonic Altar are a sacred book, a square, and a compass. These three items are considered "Masonic Lights," and every lodge is required to have them.

Why is Freemasonry satanic? Every member must achieve all the rituals to become a third degree or Master Mason. During the third degree ritual, the member is baptized unto Satan. This satanic baptism and allegiance to Lucifer is hidden from the initiate, and they are given some story about an obscure character named Hiram Abiff (who the initiate role plays in a little drama) that is killed by some ruffians, and then "raised" up to be reburied at a proper location. This is where the term "raised" to the third degree comes from. Only after I had repented and demitted from Freemasonry did the Holy Spirit reveal to me the real baptism behind the ritual of the third degree.

At the end of the Masonic third degree ritual, the initiate is symbolically "raised" from the dead and reburied. When he is pulled up from the floor by the Worshipful Master, he is raised on what is called the five points of fellowship. These five points seem to be symbolically connected to the five-pointed star, or Lucifer.

Remember, the Worshipful Master represents Lucifer in flesh. It is the Worshipful Master who raises the initiate "foot to foot," "knee to knee," "breast to breast," "hand to back," and "mouth to ear." These five points on the initiate's body are made to touch the exact five points on the Worshipful Master's body. This is what Freemasonry refers to as the five points of fellowship. This symbolizes the initiate's new covenant with Satan.

The initiate is being "baptized" into Lucifer while acting as the obscure character Hiram Abiff. He is killed, buried, and raised again. This is a false baptism. The true baptism is in our savior, when symbolically we die to our old nature by being immersed in water, and are then raised as new creatures in our savior when coming out of the water.

In the ritual of the third degree, the Master Mason is lifted by a lion's paw grip from the floor by the Worshipful Master, and the five body parts touch. Here is what they represent ritualistically as the initiate is completely baptized in Lucifer.

1. Foot to Foot means the initiate is "walking to," "standing with," or "running toward" Lucifer and all that is in his kingdom of the world.

2. Knee to Knee means the initiate is "bowing his knee" in worship to Satan.

3. Breast to Breast means the initiate is "giving his heart" to Satan.

4. Hand to Back means the initiate is to "labor by putting the back into the work, or being fervent in the duties of Satan's kingdom.

5. Mouth to Ear means the initiate should be obedient to the commands of Satan by "listening to the words" of Satan.

Earlier, I described both the interior of that particular church, and the interior of any Masonic temple. Now we shall compare the two for additional insight. First, both the church building and Masonic temples face the east. The large glass panes at the east of the church building allowed the rays of the rising sun to emanate through the sanctuary. The glass panes function the same way that the lighted emblem of the Blazing Star pentagram in the Masonic lodge does. The panes represented the Blazing Star or Lucifer.

Second, standing in front of the glass panes at the east of the church's interior was its pastor. Just like the Worshipful Master in the lodge who stands and sits in the east of the lodge under the Blazing Star. Both are the leaders and set the tone of its assembly. Both represent something bigger than themselves.

Third, on either side of the pastor stood two Greco-Roman columns, just like the Masonic Greco-Roman columns of Jachin and Boaz. Fourth, in front of the pastor were steps leading to an altar, as in the Masonic lodge. The church assembly, like the Masonic initiate, would go worship at this altar, and receive impartations of demons from others. Fifth, just as in Freemasonry the members of the organization enter through a west door. Both the church's interior and the interior of a Masonic lodge require its members to enter the temple through the west door.

But, unlike the Masonic lodge, the church took its paganism one step further by supplying two decorated and cared for graven idols in the form of cherub angels to watch over its congregation as they partied at the altar! Did no one notice this was in direct violation of the second commandment of God? Exodus 20:4, 5 demands, "Thou shalt not make any graven image, or any likeness of anything that is in heaven above, or that is in the earth beneath, or that is in the water under the earth: Thou shalt not bow down thyself to them, nor serve them, for I the Lord thy God am a jealous God, visiting the iniquity of the fathers upon the children of them that hate me."

Finally, the overall geometric shape of the church's interior presented itself as an overlay of a Masonic square and a Masonic compass. That shape along with the sacred book placed on the pastor's podium, were equal to the required items in every Masonic lodge, the three lights of Freemasonry.

Almost anyone can understand that Freemasonry and its symbolism are completely evil. So why would a church building be built around such symbolism? Was the architect a Mason? Was the owner of the construction company, which built the sanctuary involved with Freemasonry? We may never know, but we can be sure that this particular example is just one in many across the nation.

Not that there are many church buildings that resemble Masonic temples, rather that many churches participate in the occult worship of another deity when they believe they are serving the all mighty God. It does not matter what the building resembles, it is the content and context of the inside worship that matters. If a church body or its Christianity is built on false plans, a deceptive architecture, and a spiritually pagan foundation, then it is not of God. This is the lesson God wished to impart to us on that Sunday morning when our eyes were opened to see unseen enemies.

Chapter 4: Nothing Will Harm You

It bothered us immensely to be afraid while attending church services. At first, it was a difficult thing to understand; calling on the blood of Yeshua for protection when going into a supposedly "house of God." We realized that it was in "the church" where the demons operated. There is no better place for the enemy to deceive, entrap, and destroy God's children. This fact also applies to other types of "ministries." Demons can and do operate among Christian organizations, and they are not only relegated to the organized assembly of Christians in a church building.

Now, we wish to share something good with you. It is about the power and authority we all have in Christ Yeshua if we live under his covenant in obedience to him. This is something mature Christians know, but often the enemy wants us to believe otherwise and distracts us from this great truth.

In the middle of the night, I heard a song in my sleep. It was an old hymn, "Jesus, Jesus, Jesus, sweetest name I know. He fills my every longing, and keeps me singing as I go." Then I had a thought that something bad was about to happen, and it would be the reason I would need that song. I immediately awoke (3:05 AM), and looked around the room. I did not see or feel anything rather I felt the need to pray over Linda. So, I placed my hand on her head and prayed over her. No big deal, we do this to one another all the time. I then fell back into a peaceful sleep.

Then I had a dream. I dreamed Linda and I were alone in a dark gray prison building. I had three DVDs in my hand, and I was telling Linda that each producer or director of these DVDs had been involved in some sort of occult activity well before producing their major works, which deceptively promoted their satanic philosophies. One of the DVDs had been produced by a woman, who had endorsed and embraced "scientology" before becoming a famous film director. The point was that these people did not just appear out of thin air, but had been involved in occult deception long before they became famous.

Linda and I were discussing this revelation when I told her that I had to go down to the basement to do something (I don't know what) with the DVDs. She was adding valuable insight to my discovery, and I asked her to accompany me to the basement. She said, "I better stay and make coffee." But, I begged her to go with me. We held hands and talked as we walked past empty jail cells and down to the basement.

Once in the basement I bent down on my right knee to do whatever I was to do with the DVDs, while Linda stood to my right side facing a large empty projection screen. I looked up at her and saw that she was staring at the screen, stiff, paralyzed, and unable to speak or move. I knew an evil spirit had descended upon her and was holding her captive.

I tried to reach out to her but could barely crawl. I thought, "This can't happen to us, we are Christians." But it was happening. Linda with eyes wide open, paralyzed, began to topple backwards. I crawled to her and broke her fall saying, "I got you, I got you." I gently placed her head on the floor. And I was frightened because she was stiff like a zombie with her real self trapped inside an unresponsive body.

Kneeling beside her, I began to quickly repeat the following yell three times. I cried out, "Yeshua, get here right now!" The second yell, "Yeshua, come here now!" And the third cry was, "Yeshua, come down here right now!" In my dream, Yeshua was as real as any living human being was. He was like a paramedic waiting on the floor above me to answer my summons for immediate help. It was unlike normal praying, or rebuking evil in the name of our savior. It was as if Yeshua was a real living man, and I was yelling for him. I was screaming for him to get down to the basement immediately! This was an emergency, and we needed his help urgently.

At my third yell, Linda (in real life, not in the dream) woke me up from this realistic and frightening experience. Can you see Yeshua coming to our rescue by using Linda in reality to wake me? Obviously, I was startled, and I immediately began telling her about my experience with both the song and the dream.

Now both fully awake, Linda told me that she had felt me place my hands on her and pray over her. She was aware that I did this. She said that at 3:36 AM, she awoke from her sleep and looked over at me, as I was sleeping facing her. All seemed fine. Then she heard me blow a few puffs of air and start to groan. She reached over to rub my arm and felt it chillingly cold with goose bumps all over. She knew something was wrong, and she immediately woke me up. This was the exact moment of my last cry to Yeshua, "Get here now!" He literally got there "now."

While still lying in bed, Linda felt a dark presence attempting to hover over her and descend upon her. As an immediate reaction, she physically threw an arm up over her face to block the evil. She believed it wanted to manifest itself over her causing a stupor, fear, and chaos just like the drama in my dream. I asked her if she was feeling all right, and she told me of the evil presence above her. So, we both calmly and authoritatively reminded the evil presence of the authority which Yeshua our Lord had given us over it. We removed it in the authority of our Lord, and all was fine. No screaming, kicking, yelling, or struggle was needed in this case. All we needed was the calm, cool, and very real authority of our savior he had given us over demons.

As we both fell back into a peaceful sleep, God reminded me that he is always in control. God is always in control of all things. Nothing occurs without his permission, and that he is always ready to respond to our cry of, "Get here now!" Mature Christians know that God allows our buttons to be pushed at times, testing us for character and fruit, growing us in his image. This is how we are sanctified and become like our savior. We never lose sight of the fact that we always depend on our Lord.

We made a very interesting discovery the following morning. For years, every night before going to sleep, one of us picks up any dog food bowls from the floor because we do not want "visitors" in the night (mice, bugs, etc.). However, on the night of the dream, we forgot to do this. So, in the morning Linda picked up a dog food bowl, and discovered a dead and crushed scorpion underneath! It appeared to have been trampled and smashed to death. How did it get there? What could have crushed it? We laughed at the humorous implication of that object lesson. The night before we had experienced real evil, prayed to God, and the evil was crushed in the authority of Yeshua. Now we were seeing a real manifestation of a crushed scorpion in our home just as Yeshua told his disciples would happen.

In the gospel of Luke chapter ten, there were 70 disciples returning from their first missionary trip after receiving authority from Yeshua to preach the gospel, heal the sick, and cast out demons. They were exuberant on their return because of the authority granted them to conduct these miracles (the casting out of demons is a miracle). They said, "Lord, even the demons obey us!" Yeshua replied, "I saw Satan fall like lightening. Look, I give you authority to trample on serpents and scorpions and over all the power of the enemy, and nothing (and I mean nothing) by any means can harm you."

We certainly had an object lesson in front of us. But, our God is merciful; he could have used a trampled snake! However, God knew that a small crushed, trampled, and dead scorpion located under a dog food bowl would be enough to allow the lesson to be understood. We could handle that.

Some of our object lessons and experiences allowed by God to thrust us in new directions were not so pleasant even though the outcome was a blessing. Linda will write the following sections from her perspective regarding God's ability to use "high strangeness" to keep us safe from harm, and to keep us away from the path of deception. If we as Christians will listen to the voice and leading of the Holy Spirit, he will guide us to all truth in all matters. Even with the truth that many of our modern churches are apostate and deceived, God will keep all his children safe from deception if we will listen and obey his words.

Several years ago, my husband Paul had a thriving ministry on an Internet video channel. His goal was to reach the lost and unsaved by presenting the gospel of our savior in unique ways. One of these ways in starting dialogue with others was to use various U.F.O. reports and information about aliens, abductions, mutilations, and flying craft from around the globe. As he became involved in the alien information world, I also became interested.

We subscribed to several newsletters and podcasts from "Christian experts" on U.F.O. activity. We thought it was safe because the information came from Christian sources. These Christian alien experts sold books and DVDs giving a mixed message. One, they believed the

U.F.O. phenomena was evil and demonic, and second, they encouraged the study of it.

Before long, Paul had captured several U.F.O. pictures and video using a digital camera while we were just outside walking the dogs or relaxing under the open sky. These were solid metallic appearing flying craft, which only appeared after the photos or videos had been downloaded to a computer. At first, this was exciting to capture unidentified crafts on a digital camera. Paul even found a mutilated coyote on our property with its blood drained, and sporting a perfectly round hole between its shoulder blades. So, our interest in aliens, mutilations, abductions, and structured flying craft began to increase.

Paul was now filming everywhere we went in order to capture on camera strange phenomena. Then one evening, he was outside and saw some lights in the distance. After determining that the lights were not of an earthly origin, he ran inside to get me so I could see the potential U.F.O. When I went outside, I saw the lights, but I did not feel right. I felt a strange and weird feeling come over me, as if we should not be looking at this thing. I went back inside, leaving Paul there to study this craft.

Paul spent a long time outside filming the night sky. He saw nothing more with the naked eye, but when he downloaded the digital file to his computer, he saw a strange pulsating craft he believed to be a U.F.O. He quickly posted this on the Internet. Over the next several days, Paul would spend hours outside filming the heavens looking for craft.

At one point, he had "missing time," and could not remember exactly how long he had been outside, or how many days he had been U.F.O. hunting. He was becoming obsessed with documenting U.F.O. phenomena, and even considered becoming a certified investigator for a major organization that documents and investigates U.F.O. sightings.

During this time, there were several weird occurrences at night while we slept. First, Paul had a terrifying nightmare of being abducted from our bedroom. He dreamed that alien hands were dragging him from our bed and out of the window into the night sky. He was horrified upon awakening.

Second, I heard a female voice call my name while I slept. She called out to me in a long drawn out whisper with a hint of a hissing sound, "Linnnnnnn-Daaaaaaa." I felt no fear, and I had the distinct impression that this entity would return to present me with a gift; a gift of enlightenment. This appeared to be a good thing because I had been praying for more godly insight and wisdom. Yet, I was somewhat puzzled and hesitant, because I was not certain this voice with its gift were from God.

Here is the key to interpreting "experiences," always be cautious and hesitant and wait until the experience or revelation legitimately lines up with the word of God contained in the Scriptures. Recall that the vision of the sloth and of the temple of the sun were confirmed and verified by many Scriptures. Those experiences were not relating something that the Scriptures did not already state. When having a supernatural experience, take a neutral approach praying to God for interpretation using his Scriptures. If the experience is from God, it will be verified through the written word of God. If the experience is of Lucifer, than confusion, fear, doubt, and an anti-Biblical message will be forthright.

After hearing the female voice and having the impression of a gift of enlightenment, I told Paul about the experience the following morning. He asked me if I had felt fear, or an evil nature about the voice, which I answered that I had not felt anything sinister about the experience. He advised that we stay neutral about it, and to wait upon the Lord to reveal anything further. I had the attitude that if the voice were from God, he would confirm it.

The third and final event occurred just two days after I had heard the female voice while I slept. Paul and I went to sleep, and sometime during the night, Paul suddenly struck me hard on the chest area, waking me up in a panic. I looked at him and screamed while he was looking at me screaming! We were both under intense debilitating fear. Once we composed ourselves, Paul said to me, "I heard her; she called out your name!" All of a sudden, our bedroom filled with this ice-cold fear, and I felt sick to my stomach that Paul heard a demonic voice actually call out my name.

Paul said that while he slept, he felt a dark brooding presence floating above him. He then heard very distinctly and clearly a female voice. The voice was extremely breathy and hissing saying, "Linnnnnnn-Daaaaaaa," with the emphasis on the last syllable of my name. That is when he felt such fear he threw his arm up in the air and it came crashing down on me, waking both of us in shear panic and fright. We both knew now that this voice was not godly, and the gift it wanted to give me was something I did not want.

We both realized that we had opened ourselves up to demonic attacks through the U.F.O. and alien connection. The more Paul obsessed with aliens, the closer he became to experiencing abductions by demonic spirits. Likewise, the more I studied U.F.O. phenomena, the closer I came to being demonized by unclean spirits. We both repented and asked God for forgiveness.

We had subtly allowed a slow demonic deception to creep into our lives. Although, we knew better than to be deceived and had studied spiritual warfare along with experiencing demonic attacks. Yet, we fell for a sly deception believing aliens or U.F.O. phenomena could be anything other than demons doing their dirty work. This was a valuable lesson and quite a teaching moment for us.

Paul deleted all U.F.O. pictures, videos, and documentation. He unsubscribed to all "Christian alien experts," and finally took down his Internet video ministry because of the content. The obsession to film the skies left him, and we have never been plagued with alien-demons since. Repentance means turning away from the error. We had to get out of Babylon. The lesson for us was simple.

A Biblical Christian must stay alert and sober. A Biblical Christian must take heed and pay attention to everything going on around them. Test all the spirits constantly, even when they come from a Christian source. And of course, the best protection a Biblical Christian can have is to live under God's moral and ethical law, obeying and fulfilling our part in God's covenant.

Let me explain this further. We recently viewed a website that promised anyone would be able to "hear God," guaranteed, by purchasing and enrolling in their three-day course, which would teach you how to be still and hear God. The website is run by a Dr. so-n-so who is an expert at this-n-that, and boldly proclaims, "Not a study about God, but encounters with God." Ugh! How much more new-age Christian metaphysical mystical nonsense are we going to tolerate?

To declare a purpose to "not study God," but rather, "encounter or experience God," is the same old Gnostic lie repackaged. This is a lie from Lucifer, "Surely God did not say this-n-that, surely God's word is void, rather experience wisdom and gnosis, and be as the gods!" It started for us humans in Genesis chapter three. And Dr. "Cultural Christian" continues to babble this satanic lie from the father of all lies with many deceived ignorant church members buying into it; literally and allegorically.

We are going to say this over again because we say it all the time, but few have the spiritual sense to listen. We can only hope that people will "get it" by the time they are finished reading this book. Understanding the following will prevent you or someone you know from going to hell fire after death.

If you want to encounter God, if you want God to manifest himself to you, then you have to KEEP HIS COMMANDMENTS, period! Listen, you cannot use this mystical metaphysical witchcraft to manipulate and summon the Most High God into your life. You will summon a little "g" god demon to take residence in your ignorant soul, but that is about it, plus you will be a few dollars poorer.

So, no matter who recommends this-n-that book, or this-n-that website, or this-n-that speaker, do not go the way of Eve in the Garden of Eden. God's word is the only word you need to manifest the only true creator God of the universe.

Notice the following Scripture is taken from God's word spoken by God himself while he was manifested in human form. Notice that the first criteria to be filled prior to God manifesting to a person is to keep his commandments, not just have them! It is vital and essential to obey God's commandments. Obedience is the action verb to the subject, commandments. How hard is this to understand?

Yeshua said, "He that hath my commandments, and keepeth them, he it is that loveth me: and he that loveth me shall be loved of my Father, and I will love him, and will manifest myself to him." (John 14:21). All other ways to God's manifestations are false.

A good example of a church attempting to manipulate God's presence is a church that arranges its interior to the principles of the ancient Chinese art of Feng Shui for the purposes of building a better subtle energy spirit. Not too long ago, a man contacted us regarding a question he had about his church using Feng Shui. He wanted to know if it was Biblical to subscribe to such beliefs. The sad thing is he had to seek an answer from someone else on this topic instead of knowing the answer based on his own study of the word of God. The second disgusting thing was his church practicing this pagan ritual to achieve a higher God consciousness.

Feng Shui (pronounced Fung Shway) is an ancient form of Chinese divination. It is not a martial art or fighting art, but uses the same principles of "chi" energy, ying and yang, and philosophical Taoism. Feng Shui means literally "wind water," and is part of an ancient Chinese philosophy of nature. The analogy of wind and water is used, because an obstruction of either wind or water causes it to change its movement and break its natural motion. It is a form of geomancy and divination by geographic features. The practice of Feng Shui purposes to use the energy of the environment to bring harmony to the individual impacted by that space. It relates to the idea that living with, rather than against, nature benefits both humans and the environment.

Alleged masters of Feng Shui are supposed to be able to detect metaphysical energies and give directions for their optimal flow in any given space or environment. Much like Chinese acupuncture for the body, Feng Shui redirects energies in a person's home, office, or neighborhood (and now the church). These wizards and sorcerers are invited into buildings and landscapes, using their metaphysical abilities to detect the flow of good and bad "energy." Feng Shui masters using their "gifts" declare where bathrooms should go, which way doorways should face, where mirrors should hang, which room needs green plants and which one needs red flowers. They decide these things based on their feel for the flow of chi energies, which are electromagnetic fields or whatever other form of energy they sense.

American Corporations have employed Feng Shui consultants to create more psychologically friendly office spaces and reception areas. Often the masters, called specialists or diviners, use compass-like instruments to determine the exact cosmic forces touching a site. Appropriate sites are chosen in relation to bodies of water and mountains. Feng Shui, especially as it affects interior design, has recently become popular in Britain and America. Many major book retailers carry "do-it-yourself" Feng Shui books teaching the reader basic techniques to arrange furniture, mirrors, crystals, and fountains to enhance the positive energy in their homes or offices, and of course now some neo-pagan churches.

Feng Shui is witchcraft. It is the occult manipulation of the environment using spiritual entities, and is not compatible with Biblical Christianity. The sense of flow and natural movement of the "wind water" energy was originally attributed to spirits. Furniture or architecture would obstruct spiritual entities, causing blockage and a feeling of anxiety. However, Feng Shui consultants now try to explain the spiritual concepts in terms Christians, homeowners, and church organizations will understand. In other words, the original belief that spiritual entities cause harm to a person within a particular environment has been hidden in order to sell this ancient form of witchcraft.

The same applies to Yoga in the church. There is no such thing as "Christian Yoga." It is impossible to separate Hinduism from the practice of Yoga. Any Hindu Yoga master will tell you this is true! However, our blind and deaf Cultural Christianity continues to implement such far eastern practices like Yoga, mediation, and contemplative prayer into the church body. The very word Yoga means to "yoke with the deity," or "become one with the deity."

Believe us, it is not the God of the Bible that one is becoming yoked to in this satanic pose practice. The poses or stretches are designed to worship the Hindu devils. Yoga has been sold to the west as a form of exercise, but it is not exercise, it is worship of demonic deities. We wrote about Yoga and the martial arts in our eBook, "Martial Arts: A Biblical Perspective," which goes into detail about the compatibility of these practices with Biblical Christianity. The following is an excerpt from that book.

"Another area where this ancient idea of moving energy through the body to achieve power and well being is found in fitness and health programs. Remember, that an ancient monk from India came to China, teaching monks yogic meditation for the improvement of health and fitness. These standing yogic movements are what evolved into the fighting arts, which we know as the martial arts. The root is the same.

In fact, yogic exercises are taught to the elderly as well as to the young. Businesses and corporate America have embraced meditation and Yoga as beneficial stress relievers. I have seen many 'Christian' DVDs and books about practicing Yoga.

These instructors believe if they change the names of the pagan poses to Biblical names and if they meditate on our savior rather than empty the mind, then it will be safe to practice this ancient form of idol worship. What is in a pose or posture? Well, the poses are representative of various pagan rituals and demon worship. So, even if a Christian changes the names and 'Christianizes' them, they are still rooted in an ancient philosophy of paganism.

For example, the yogic posture of the 'sun salutation' is just one of many basic moves in this practice. A Christian may replace the term 'Sun' with the word 'Son' and do the salute to Yeshua. However, this does not change the root of this pose. Yoga.com, a non-Christian website dedicated to all things Yoga, has this to say about the salutation.

'The sun is God . . . giver of life to all beings. In India, the sunrise is thought of as the eye of God . . .people acknowledge God with a moving prayer called Surya Namaskara, sun salutation.' So, any Biblical Christian can see that performing the sun salutation is bowing down in worship to the sun god, which is not our Biblical creator God. Yoga.com continues, 'This worship includes prayer to the sun . . .each posture corresponds to the twelve signs of the zodiac . . .making it a ritual to honor the sun and receive physical and

spiritual energy through sun salutations and chanting can transform our lives.'

The word Yoga means 'union with the one.' Union with what one I ask. All these people practicing this ancient idolatry and demon worship walk around in Yoga class and greet one another with the word, 'Namaste.' The definition of Namaste is 'both a physical gesture and a spoken spiritual salutation, which is the recognition of the divine spirit (or soul) in another by the divine spirit in you.'

This definition of Namaste is according to livingwordsofwisdom.com. The physical part of 'bowing to the divine' in another person consists of placing the hands together in front of the third eye chakra and then moving them in front of the heart chakra. Additionally, just saying the word Namaste at the beginning of meditation allegedly assists the practitioner to go deeper into their divine heart center, and access the flow of divine love for others. Other ways of understanding Namaste are, 'The god/goddess in me acknowledges the god/goddess in you.' My question is, 'What divine being are people acknowledging and worshipping?' My God is the creator God of the ancient Scriptures, not the created sun or any other little 'g' god.

Are there dangers in practicing Yoga? Yes, just like the dangers of any meditation, yogic practices can bring some real harm to the practitioner. In an online article, Kundalini Yoga Dangers, at buzzle.com, there are several severe dangers associated with this particular form of Yoga. Listed are several unpleasant side effects such as, body pain, burning and inflammation, hypersensitivity to heat and cold, drastic changes in appetite, fluctuating sexual energies and drives, unexpected negative symptoms of guilt, depression, anxiety, and confusion. Interestingly, we seldom hear about the negative side effects of yogic or martial arts meditative practices."

Another mystic practice that is sweeping the carnal church by storm is contemplative prayer or meditation prayer. Contemplation was vital within the philosophy of Plato. Through contemplation, Plato believed, the soul could ascend to the knowledge of the "form of the good" or other divine forms. Additionally, Plato said the highest contemplation was a critical component in order to reach the experience of oneness, unity, or the vision of a god. It is believed that Plato experienced this experience four times. The origins of contemplative prayer are contained in the Greek mystery religions that parallel the far eastern philosophies of India and China. Plato's experience of "oneness" with a deity is the same as Yoga's claim to "yoke" its practitioners with a deity.

Contemplative prayer assists one to enter an altered state of consciousness to find the practitioner's true self, and through the process, they believe they find God. Proponents of contemplative prayer believe and teach a false doctrine, which states that all human beings have a divine center and that all, not just born again believers, should practice contemplative prayer exercises in order to spark that divine center. Make no mistake about it; meditative prayer uses ancient mystical practices to induce altered states of consciousness just like any other pagan mystic practice. The mind is emptied, and the ignorant Christian opens up their spirit to demonic infestation. The practice is often couched in Christian jargon and terminology, but it is not a Biblical practice.

Chapter 5: Living in Covenant

When we speak of living under the covenant, we are referring to obedience and faith in God's moral law as contained within the Ten Commandments, or to the ten stipulations of the agreement between God and us. We are not advocating placing anyone under the civil or ceremonial laws written for ancient Israel before the laws were fulfilled in Yeshua our savior. We are not talking about the ritual sacrifice of blood from goats and bulls, rather about the obedience and trust in God's moral law. His moral law is unchanging, and it is just as applicable today as it was for ancient Israel.

The Apostle Paul often wrote against the burden of the ceremonial law, and freed his readers from ritualistic temple system activities. However, the uses of the word "law" in these writings never refer to God's moral or ethical law. These are the laws written on our hearts of flesh through the salvation received through the faith in Yeshua our savior. Yeshua distilled God's entire moral law into two statements. First, love God with all your heart, soul, and mind, and second; love your neighbor as yourself. (Matthew 22:37-40).

If we as Biblical Christians live under covenant, then we will be delivered from deception no matter what type of church one is attending. If we attend a godly church, then living under covenant will greatly bless and enrich the lives of others surrounding us. If we attend a neo-pagan church, then living under covenant will convict us of the error and drive us out from her.

Now, let us make a detailed examination of the ten stipulations of God's covenant.

In Exodus chapter 20, God declares to Israel that he alone is their God, and that he alone was the only God that brought them out of Egypt, which is likened to a house of bondage. The symbolism of "the house of bondage" can be applied to our Christian salvation when our savior brought us out of the system of worldly slavery under sin. Additionally, it can refer to the end of time when God finally destroys all evil and brings us into a new eternal land of freedom. The important thing to remember is that God is the one who delivers, and no other deity is to be credited with that miracle. It is because God alone is the deliverer that a covenant is made between two parties. Obedience to the stipulations bring blessings, and disobedience to the stipulations bring curses as outlined in Deuteronomy chapters 28 through 30.

First Three Stipulations

"Thou shalt have no other gods before me." (Exodus 20:3). We must not have any little "g" gods instead of, or in replacement of the only God. This stipulation can be violated if we do not take heed of what is taking precedence before our God. This violation can entail worship of your children, spouse, family, church, occupation, or religion. It can easily be violated when we place the "lord of the work" before the "work of the Lord." Remember how my husband Paul had the obsession of U.F.O. and alien studies placed alongside his worship of God, and the results of that inappropriate worship.

"Thou shalt not make unto thee any graven image, or any likeness of anything that is in heaven above, or that is in the earth beneath, or that is in the water under the earth. Thou shalt not bow down to them, nor serve them." (Exodus 20:4). Making an image also can be accomplished in your mind as in "imagination." The key to remember is that the image is served or worshipped.

"Thou shalt not take the name of the Lord thy God in vain, for he will not hold him guiltless that taketh his name in vain." (Exodus 20:7). The stipulation means that we must not represent God in a worthless manner, in emptiness, or bring reproach to his reputation (his name). We must not be guilty of using his glory for our gain because we will not be exempt from punishment. Violating the first two stipulations automatically brings shame on God's reputation because of worthless, deceitful, and empty worship of other gods or images.

Cultural Christians do not believe they are violating these three stipulations because they sincerely think they are worshipping God, but they are approaching him in an inappropriate manner. They often worship a false Yeshua, instead of the true Christ of the Bible. Ancient Israel made and worshipped a golden calf that was, in their mind, God. The golden calf was not another god to them, but it was, as they believed, the god that brought them out of Egypt! When Cultural Christians violate the first two stipulations, they automatically violate the third by bringing shame and reproach on the name and character of God.

In part two of this book, we will go into greater detail about these first commandments, and teach you how to destroy those idols that may be present in your life. Again, these idols are unseen enemies that must be exposed and eliminated. Killing these idols is part of obedience to God's word, and result in living Biblical Christianity.

The Fourth Stipulation

"Remember the Sabbath day, to keep it holy. Six days shalt thou labor, and do all thy work, but in the seventh day is the Sabbath of the Lord thy God: in it, thou shalt not do any work. For in six days the Lord made heaven and earth, the sea, and all that in them is, and rested the seventh day: Wherefore the Lord blessed the Sabbath day and hallowed it." (Exodus 20:8-11). Christians have all sorts of ideas and misconceptions about the fourth commandment. Most ignore it, because they do not understand it, or place them and others under the ceremonial law of observing Saturday worship with no other activity allowed. We propose to do neither. First, let us dissect the meaning behind keeping the Sabbath holy.

Why is the separation of the seventh day from the other six days important to God? Because "In six days the Lord made heaven and earth, the sea, and all that in them is, and rested the seventh day, wherefore he blessed the Sabbath day, and hallowed it." Because God labored for six days in creating the earth, and ceased from his labor on the seventh day, he separated (made holy) that seventh day from the other six.

Thus, reflection and remembrance of the seventh day is tied into God's creation of the cosmos, and into his rest after the labor associated with our material universe. God rested, and he wants us to rest because at the end of the age, when all wickedness on earth is destroyed, we will all rest in God's new heaven and new earth. So, the Sabbath observance is prophetic! Taking a day off from all our regular labors to reflect, recall, and remember God's mighty works in creation and the mighty works he will do in the new re-creation is all he is asking us to do. A simple observance and reflection is all that is required.

In Deuteronomy chapter five, the reason stated for separating the seventh day from the other six was so Israel could recall or remember what God had done for them. "That thou was a servant in the land of Egypt, and that the Lord thy God brought thee out thence through a mighty hand and a stretched out arm: Therefore the Lord thy God commanded thee to keep the Sabbath day." (Deuteronomy 5:12-15).

The same commandment of repose and reflection on the mighty works of God are contained in Deuteronomy as well as in Exodus. It too is prophetic! Just as God rescued, delivered, and "brought out" his people from the land of bondage and slavery, he will also one day rescue, deliver, and "bring out" his Ecclesia from the satanic bondage of this present worldly system of Lucifer. Thus, the command to keep the Sabbath holy is no more than taking a day off from the "matrix" of satanic bondage and work, and reflecting on the great works of God in our behalf, both in the past and in the future. It is possessing what we refer to as, "The eternal mind."

Ancient Israel, as well as the early church of the first century believed that our current world operating under the fallen angel Lucifer, would last six thousand years, and then would be destroyed along with all evil at the end of that period. The final thousand-year period, after the destruction of Satan's kingdom, would be the millennial Sabbath rest. One can understand the symbolism of six-days of labor and the seventh-day of rest. Just as God labored for six days in creating the cosmos, and then rested, we will labor for six thousand years before finding rest from our servitude. This is the end of the age, or the end of time.

An early first century letter that circulated among the early church had the title, "Epistle of Barnabas." This letter is not in our canonized Bible, but exists in revealing some important concepts and teachings of first century Christianity. We quote it here only to demonstrate the thinking of some in the early church regarding the Sabbath.

The writer of the Epistle of Barnabas explains his concept of God's Sabbath as outlined in the Ten Commandments. "He speaketh, too, of the Sabbath in the beginning of the creation: And God made in six days the works of his hands, and finished them on the seventh day, and rested in it and sanctified it. Consider, my children, what signify the words, he finished them in six days. They mean this: that in six thousand years the Lord will make an end of all things, for a day is with him as a thousand years. And he himself beareth witness unto me, saying: Behold this day a day shall be as a thousand years. Therefore, my children, in six days, that is in six thousand years, shall all things be brought to an end. And the words, he rested on the seventh day, signify this: After that his Son hath come, and hath caused to cease the time of the wicked one, and hath judged the ungodly, and changed the sun and the moon and the stars, then shall he rest well on the seventh day." (Barnabas 15:3-6).

In support of Barnabas' commentary are many Scriptures, which state that the Sabbath is a "sign," "omen," or "mark" to be observed. The question is, "What is the Sabbath pointing to, if not eternal rest?" Exodus 31:13-17 twice refers to the Sabbath as a sign. Ezekiel chapter 20 refers to the Sabbath twice as being a sign. In Leviticus chapter 25, the Sabbath is referred to as "years" rather than "days" when commanding a seventh year rest for the land. The book of Hebrews chapter four contains teaching about the Sabbath rest, "For he that is entered into his rest, he also hath ceased from his own works, as God did from his." Perhaps, the period of seven thousand years from creation to the Sabbath rest is mentioned in Revelation chapter 20. If the millennium rest is a thousand year span, then it is logical to assume that it is preceded by a six thousand year span of labor.

When referring to a millennial thousand-year Sabbath, the writer of the Epistle of Barnabas states, "For a day is with him as a thousand years." We find Scriptural support in Psalms 90:4, "For a thousand years in thy sight are but as yesterday when it is past, and as a watch in the night." Additionally, 2Peter 3:8 admonishes us, "But, beloved be not ignorant of this one thing, that one day is with the Lord as a thousand years, and a thousand years as one day."

We heard a pastor say that Biblical prophecy should be left to the theological wizards. This church leader refused to teach his congregation anything about God's prophetic plan, but instead wallowed in feel-good motivational self-help sermons, which gave him much adoration from his followers. This is a violation in not recalling the Sabbath rest and separating it from everything else. We must take a rest from our labors to contemplate God's redemptive prophetic plan. We are to remember all of God's mighty works both in the past and in the future. We are commanded in the fourth stipulation to have an "eternal mind." The book of Revelation 20:10 declares, "For the testimony of Yeshua is the spirit of prophecy."

The Fifth through the Tenth Stipulations

The above stipulations are all God centered with the remaining stipulations neighbor centered. This is why Yeshua said all the law and all the prophets could hang on two commands; love your God with everything you have, and love your neighbor. With true Biblical love toward God and others, the rest of the commandments fall into place.

"Honor thy father and thy mother that thy days may be long upon the land, which the Lord thy God giveth thee." (Exodus 20:12). Part of a discourse on treating others correctly is found in Ephesians chapter six. The

Apostle Paul explains, "Children obey your parents in the Lord, for this is right. Honor thy father and mother, which is the first commandment with promise, that it may be well with thee, and thou mayest live long on the earth."

"Thou shalt not kill." (Exodus 20:13). The Hebrew word translated kill is murder, slay, assassinate, or to dash in pieces. Yeshua taught that if a person hates his brother, it is the same as murder in his heart. Most Cultural Christians do not have a problem with murder, but may have hatred toward others with a lack of forgiveness.

"Thou shalt not commit adultery." (Exodus 20:14). The meaning behind the primitive root word that is translated adultery can also mean to figuratively apostatize. An adulterer is one who breaks the vows of wedlock and has sexual relations with a man not her husband. Throughout Scripture, God calls one who worships and serves idols an adulterer. It is the breaking of his covenant and relationship as husband, Lord, and master. All Israel were the wife of God, and the true called-out-ones are the bride of Christ. Thus, we can faithfully say that the Cultural Christian church serving a false Yeshua is committing spiritual adultery and being a whore. Anything less or more than true Biblical Christianity is a violation of this seventh commandment.

"Thou shalt not steal." (Exodus 20:15). The implication behind the Hebrew root word translated steal is "deceit." To steal is to deceive, or to carry away by stealth. The punch behind this commandment is the order to be honest with others. Many neo-pagan churches today preach a prosperity gospel to deceive the sheep into giving away their finances to the church organization. Many preachers, speakers, and pastors manipulate the masses for their own monetary or positional gain. Any gospel preached that is not the Biblical gospel of Christ is a deception and a theft. Also, to withhold deep Biblical study and truths of God contained in the Scriptures equals "stealing" from the congregation.

"Thou shalt not bear false witness against thy neighbor." (Exodus 20:16). How many people violate this commandment when giving someone in the church a false or deceitful message allegedly from God? Perhaps they are motivated by spiritual pride when they speak a word over someone that is not from God. A false prophet or a false teacher bearing ungodly and fraudulent testimony to others is in direct violation of this ninth stipulation to God's covenant. Claiming that demonic experiences and manifestations are from God, deceiving others in the process, is bearing a false witness to the power of God. Hyper-charismatic churches operating in demonic kundalini serpent energy while claiming their manifestations are from God are false witnesses. Cold, dry, and dead churches that deny the Biblical power of the Holy Spirit also bear a false witness to others by denying the true and miraculous power of God as taught in the Scriptures.

"Thou shalt not covet...anything that is thy neighbor's." (Exodus 20:17). Lusting after something, desiring something, and taking great delight in things not our own is the meaning behind the word covet. In the post-modern-neo-pagan church, mystic experiences may be sought after, or new improved methods of connecting to God may be delightfully desired. Lusting after spiritual power is to covet. Desiring to experience new-age Gnostic philosophies disguised in the emergent church is to covet. We see many Christian organizations desiring to be famous and loved by the masses by participating in social causes such as ending slavery, hunger, or abortion while preaching a false gospel of Christ.

As we conclude this review of the Ten Commandments, and their applicability to the Biblical Christian, one can clearly understand the differences between living under covenant and being deceived in a Babylonian church organization. Understanding God's moral law and walking in them in obedience will prevent the Biblical Christian from becoming deceived and demonized while attending or participating in false Christian religions. Living under the covenant will give the Biblical Christian eyes to see unseen enemies, and open up their hearts to recognize a true and beautiful body of Christ, a remnant also living under the covenant of God.

In the following section, part two "Idolicide," we will explore the many unseen enemies of idolatry that can enslave a Christian. With eyes wide open and ready to see, you will learn to recognize those subtle lies and deceits that can easily trip up a Christian. These lessons are individual in nature, but the church is made up of individuals. If more individuals will commit to a

Biblical lifestyle, then our churches may return to true Biblical Christianity.

Paul and Linda Villanueva

PART TWO: IDOLICIDE

Killing Idols

What is idolicide? It is a word we invented to refer to the killing of idols. Idolicide is a noun, but we use it with the intent of an action verb. We want the reader to take action against the idols, which prevent a true worship of the All Mighty God in spirit and in truth, and we want the reader to destroy those idols from their lives. God has commanded, "You shall have no other gods before me." It is that simple. The command and the requirement never changed, and we all must actively seek out those idolatrous things in our lives that would prevent us from having eternal life and salvation with our Father God.

Pagan gods and goddesses are easily recognized, but are the subtle idols of attitude, behavior, or belief systems easily discerned? Anything that stands in the way between you and the All Mighty God is an idol. Together we will explore and expose the hidden idols of tradition, religion, doubt, impatience, false worship, self-pity, and much more. Together we will commit idolicide and gain new perspectives and deliverance from demonic strongholds. It is spiritual warfare. It is the beginning of battle preparation, and is foundational in living a victorious and overcoming life, a Biblical Christian life.

What you are about to read is based on Biblical Scripture alone. There are some dreams and experiences included, which point to the truth of confirming Scripture regarding committing idolicide. If you are ready to see God with deeper insight, go into a wonderful spiritual relationship, and get eyes to see, then we will begin with the following story.

Chapter 6: Pastor Pride

A friend had invited me to his church. He was so excited about this place with its charismatic pastor, and he was just as thrilled that I had agreed to attend with him. We slipped into an already in progress service and took our seats to the rear of this medium sized church building. It was not a mega-church and nothing about it or its people was extraordinary.

The pastor stood in front of his flock rather than behind a pulpit of sorts while he engaged them in colorful rhetoric and talk. I was having a difficult time listening to him because he was so arrogant. Pride dripped from him like fat from a steak, sizzling pride, and messy pride. I had my Bible open. I would rather read it than listen to the pastor's arrogant speech. I knew he noticed me. He saw one person unengaged and unimpressed.

The pastor had full control of his congregation, and I could see that he wallowed in his power over people. It was late into the night, very late. I thought, "This man keeps babbling on, keeping people here late into the night without any care or consideration to others at all." He was saying nothing of value, and only controlling others and making them sit through his arrogant speeches. But they loved him and adored him. They worshipped this man, just like my friend who brought me here idolized this pastor.

I turned around in my seat to view the clock on the wall. It was after 10 P.M. I knew this was significant and thought, "The hour is late, and these people are wasting precious time." It was a "miracle service," and anyone could receive a miracle from God on this particular night. No one else cared that it was so late, they only cared about the miracle they would receive from God via the pastor's hand.

Then a humble and contrite man came forward and stood next to Pastor Pride, his name was "Joe." I immediately thought to myself, "He represents the average Joe. His name was significant. This was the second significant sign that came to me; first, the time and now the name of Joe." Pastor Pride began questioning average Joe about what kind of miracle he wanted God to perform for him. Did he need a new job, wealth, health, love, or to just have God find his misplaced car keys?

Average Joe began to answer, and quietly said, "I want righteousness." I heard him say those words clear as a bell. Pastor Pride quickly dropped the microphone down and away so that others could not hear average Joe's request for God's righteousness. However, average Joe did ask for God's righteousness rather than for any other fancy and empty miracles.

Pastor Pride, sheepishly placing his left arm around average Joe's shoulder, said to him in the microphone for all to hear, "You already are righteous. Indeed you are." Pastor Pride did not want to address average Joe's request to repent from sin and obtain God's righteousness, rather he only wanted Joe to pick a miracle for God to "perform" in front of everyone, a miracle of show-boating, a miracle of entertainment and self glory. But Joe wanted "righteousness," so Pastor Pride told him he was already righteous and sent him away empty-handed and lost to his seat.

I was mad. I was upset at what I had just witnessed. I noticed that my friend was sitting one empty chair from me, as if he had separated himself. This was another significant observation bringing the significant signs to three: the time, average Joe, and now the empty seat of separation. I thought, "Perhaps I can talk to Joe after the service and lead him into repentance and salvation."

Suddenly a woman in the audience shouted to the pastor her miracle request. "Pastor, please have God leave day light savings time alone because I don't like the time change. Make God stop time for me because I don't like it." I just about came unglued because of this trivial, personal, God-is-my-genie-in-a-bottle request. The spiritual immaturity was overwhelming to me.

Pastor Pride wasted no time in taking the opportunity to pontificate to the woman that this request would negatively affect him. He told the audience that he planned to become an engineer upon retiring, and that the engineering field required working with precise numbers. So, stopping time would negatively affect him. That was his theological reason to not perform the miracle.

I had had enough! I looked at my friend, still seated an empty seat away from me, and firmly said, "Are you ready to go?" He bowed his head and walked out far ahead of me while I looked back to retrieve my jacket from the chair. Pastor Pride did not appreciate me standing up and leaving during his wind bagging session, and so he addressed me in front of everyone. "What are you thinking?" He shouted at me. I stopped and looked at him saying, "Brother, believe me, you don't want to know what I am thinking!"

He kept questioning me and demanding the reason for my departure. I became angered, and shouted to him, "Because you denied Joe's repentance!" He yelled back at me denying any such thing. I screamed, "Liar! I heard Joe ask for righteousness and you denied him that request."

I walked out toward the front door, but Pastor Pride kept hounding me. I knew he hated me for being independent of him. He followed me out the door. I told him that I would gladly meet him in private to discuss all the wrongs I saw because I did not wish to embarrass him in front of his church. But, I knew that that was not what he wanted. Pastor Pride squared his stance in front of me, and I knew he was about to physically attack me. He was so angry with me. With a sudden and determined leap, he charged me at full speed. His intent was to damage me as much as possible.

Strangely enough, in my right hand was a "meat cleaver" or "battle axe" type of weapon. I had no fear of this enraged demon, only anger and indignation. As he came charging toward me, I raised my right hand with its weapon knowing that when it came down on his head it would split his skull in two like a ripe melon. And I brought it down forcibly.

At that moment, my wife, Linda shouted to me, "Paul, wake up!" I woke from my dream and knew it had spiritual significance. It was time to commit idolicide and tear out the roots of evil and religious pride. The Lord God of my salvation gave me this Scripture upon awakening. "And now also the axe is laid unto the root of the trees: Therefore every tree which brings not forth good fruit is hewn down, and cast into the fire." (Mathew 3:10).

This is what having eyes to see unseen enemies is about, having the knowledge, strength and courage to commit idolicide. All idols must be destroyed, no matter how precious to the worshipper. This is not an option in a Christian's life, rather it is necessary to gain eternal salvation. "For the weapons of our warfare are not carnal, but mighty through God to the pulling down of strong holds; casting down imaginations (images and idols), and every high thing that exalts itself against the knowledge of God, and bringing into captivity every thought to the obedience of Christ; and having in a readiness to revenge all disobedience, when your obedience is fulfilled." (2Corinthians 10:4-6).

Understand your readiness or preparedness to kill/revenge all disobedient demons, spirits, idols, evil, and wickedness in your life is directly related to your fulfilling your own obedience to our savior. You cannot live a sinful life in disobedience to God's Scripture and commands while believing you can do spiritual battle to rid your life of demonic infestation. It is only after you submit your life to God through Christ in full obedience to his will, word, and commands that you can ever hope to kill the idols in your life that are causing so much pain, torment, and harassment. Idols send you to eternal damnation and are the abominations that lead to all destruction. So, it is imperative that the roots of every bad tree, not bearing good fruit, be cut out and burned with fire.

Chapter 7: Desire a Disciple's Heart

The Scriptures tell us that we should love the Lord our God with all our heart, and with all our soul, and with all our strength, and with all of our mind, and to love our neighbor as our self (Luke 10:27, Deut. 6:5, Lev 19:18). So then, what did the Lord mean in Luke 14:25-33, which reads,

"And there went great multitudes with him: and he turned, and said unto them, if any man come to me, and hate not his father, and mother, and wife, and children, and brethren, and sisters, yea, and his own life also, he cannot be my disciple. And whosoever doth not bear his cross, and come after me, cannot be my disciple. For which of you, intending to build a tower, sits not down first, and counts the cost, whether he has sufficient to finish it? Lest haply, after he hath laid the foundation, and is not able to finish it, all that behold it begin to mock him, saying, This man began to build, and was not able to finish. Or what king, going to make war against another king, sits not down first, and consults whether he is able with ten thousand to meet him that cometh against him with twenty thousand? Or else, while the other is yet a great way off, he sends an ambassador, and desires conditions of peace. So likewise, whosoever he is of you that forsakes not all that he has, he cannot be my disciple."

These passages in Scripture appear to be contradicting each other. Why would the Lord say we are to love our neighbor as our self in some passages, and then say that we cannot be his disciples unless we hate our parents, our spouse, our family, and even our own life?

Notice that all the things Christ is addressing are gifts that he has given to us. He is showing us the correct perspective of a disciple's heart. We are not to love the gifts more than we love him. He must be our first love. If we love the gifts more than the Giver of Gifts, then we are worshipping idols, which is a transgression against the commandments found in Exodus 20:1-7, which read,

"And God spoke all these words, saying, I am the Lord thy God, which have brought thee out of the land of Egypt, out of the house of bondage. Thou shall have no other gods before me. Thou shall not make unto thee any graven image, or any likeness of any thing that is in heaven above, or that is in the earth beneath, or that is in the water under the earth. Thou shall not bow down thyself to them, nor serve them: for I the Lord thy God am a jealous God, visiting the iniquity of the fathers upon the children unto the third and fourth generation of them that hate me; and showing mercy to thousands of them that love me, and keep my commandments. Thou shall not take the name of the Lord thy God in vain; for the Lord will not hold him guiltless that takes his name in vain."

Notice the generational curse that results in worshipping idols. In the New Testament, the Apostle John wrote in 1John 5:21, "Little children, guard yourselves from idols." Apostle Paul wrote in 1Corinthians 10:7, "Do not be idolaters," and in verse 14 he commands the church to "flee from idolatry." The subject of idol worship is serious. As Christ's disciples, we must heed these commands and warnings. The Scriptures warn us in Hebrews 10:31 that it is a terrifying thing to fall into the hands of the living God. There is only one true God and he is YHWH.

Father, we thank you for your word. It is our light, a lamp to our feet. Please reveal to us any idols that we may have erected and hidden in our heart. We tear down those idols in the name and authority of your son, our Lord and savior Yeshua. We repent and ask for your forgiveness. There is no other god, but you. You are the only true God. Thank you that you are faithful and just to forgive us and to cleanse us from all unrighteousness. Praise your name. Amen.

Chapter 8: Abolish Abominations

Ezekiel 16:2 states, "Son of man, cause Jerusalem to know her abominations." The words for "abominable things" in the Hebrew language, is "TOEVAH," which has the general meaning of being morally disgusting, and yet has many applications throughout Scripture. It is interesting that the use of the word is dispersed with some behaviors and practices that we find detestable today (idol worship, murder, human sacrifice, witchcraft), and others completely acceptable (homosexuality, sexual perversion, unfair business practices, lying, cheating, and disobedience). Whether we engage in such practices or simply tolerate them in our environment is not the defining line. The line is drawn in God's commands to stay away from disgusting, detestable, and abominable behaviors and practices.

Can we accept the command to avoid an abomination like murder and yet tolerate or enjoy the sexual perversion in our entertainment culture? But, one may protest, "We are not under the ceremonial law anymore." Yes, this is true, but we still ask the question, "Is it possible to accept some of the abominations and reject the others? Understand that God's moral law never changes, and we are under the law of Christ. God's commandments are still valid and necessary for all of us today. God is the same yesterday, today, and forever.

In the book of Acts, the vision that the Apostle Peter saw commanding him to eat the unclean animals was symbolic of Gentile salvation. Do we believe the Jewish Peter ate of unclean animals after he saw the vision or did he stick to his Jewish roots and avoid unclean flesh? (Acts 10:9-47). Did God become "undisgusted" with unclean flesh after the dispensation of grace was brought in through our savior Yeshua?

Can we reject the idea of making an idol to worship because it is an abomination to God, while allowing the roots of paganism found in Halloween, Easter, or Christmas celebrations to enter into our sanctuaries as harmless festivities or objects of a cultural holiday?

Will we find the thought of bloody human sacrifice to an unknown god repulsive while at the same time tolerating "Christian" homosexual and lesbian ministers in the church? Will we today tolerate and accept homosexuality as an alternative lifestyle while being disgusted at the thought of a male temple prostitute in ancient times?

Shall we cast away those who practice witchcraft and sorcery, and accept the casual reading of the daily horoscope, or become self-medicated on prescription drugs? Is the thought of burning a child alive on a pagan god's altar disgusting while at the same time accepting cheating in business, or treating others poorly as an acceptable way to climb the corporate ladder, or perhaps the organizational church ladder?

May we insist on the death penalty for the murderer and child rapist, and at the same time perjure ourselves to family and friends? Do we have permission to be arrogant, prideful, contentious, or deceitful? Is it situational, and can we justify our sin because of the situation and circumstance?

Christians are closer to committing abominations and detestable things than we realize. Mostly out of ignorance of God's word and commands. We are led astray by false doctrines. It is time to reevaluate our lives according to the commands of God having no yoke, no bondage, just understanding of the truth in God's word. We cannot, we must not, accept some things and reject other things according to our likes and dislikes. That kind of thinking is an abomination, and we must kill the idols and abominable practices if we desire to live eternally with God. "And first I will recompense their iniquity and their sin double; because they have defiled my land, they have filled mine inheritance with the carcasses of their detestable and abominable things." (Jeremiah 16:18).

In Ezekiel chapter eight, we read about the prophet Ezekiel warning the nation of Israel of impending destruction based on their worship of idols and false gods. The worship or trust in these demon-based gods is the result of their disobedience to the commands of the God of Israel. The "abominations" which the nation committed literally drove their true God away from his own sanctuary.

Passages in chapter eight depict three distinct methods in which people worship idols or place their trust in things other than God. There is no difference between the ancient nation of Israel's idol worship and our modern day lifestyle of distrusting God in our lives. The three ways of idolatry still exist.

Images that we create

Images that we imagine

Images that we submit under

The fact that God is the same yesterday, today, and forever tells us that he fervently hates with a strong passion all idol worship. God hates anything that takes away our trust and confidence in him and replaces it with a false security, pride, arrogance, strength, or belief. God will still remove himself from your sanctuary (life) if you choose to continue to distrust him.

"He said furthermore unto me, Son of man, see thou what they do, even the great abominations that the house of Israel commits here, that I should go far off from my sanctuary? But turn thee yet again, and thou shall see greater abominations." (Ezekiel 8:6).

Ezekiel saw abominations, and the first of these was related to images that were humanly created for worship. The ancients often drew or pecked images of animals, people, or other things on their walls, tombs, and temples. These images were not mere decorations, but invoked the spirit and assistance of the thing depicted. Many ancient cultures practiced this invoking of the spirits. Ezekiel peeked into a visionary hole within the temple wall, and saw the leaders of Israel worshiping or submitting themselves to the powers of demons, asking for assistance.

"So I went in and saw; and behold every form of creeping things, and abominable beasts, and all the idols of the house of Israel, portrayed upon the wall round about. And there stood before them seventy men of the ancients of the house of Israel, and in the midst of them stood Jaazaniah the son of Shaphan, with every man his censer in his hand; and a thick cloud of incense went up. Then said he unto me, Son of man, hast thou seen what the ancients of the house of Israel do in the dark, every man in the chambers of his imagery? For they say, the Lord sees us not; the Lord hath forsaken the earth." (Ezekiel 8:10-12).

The spiritual leaders secretly were placing their confidence and trust in false gods while in darkness. While on the surface they seemed legitimate and religious – they practiced demon worship in secret. The text states that they had censors and a thick cloud of incense was being offered to the drawings on the walls. Again, these were not mere drawings or paintings on a wall, but a thing created by human hands to invoke worship. The thing created represented the power of the animal or demon god. The worship always involved submission to a greater power.

The ancient Hebrews lived in an agricultural society and depended on the earth, rain, and sunshine to grow food and sustenance. They also were concerned with insects, fires, floods, and other circumstances that could destroy their food. God promised them that he would take care of them if they would live in obedience to his commands. However, when they began to assimilate pagan practices from other nations and began to believe

God had forsaken their land, they turned to trusting idols and false gods to meet their needs.

The question we must ask is how does this apply today? In what ways do you create an image representing your power, strength, assistance, sustenance, or survival? Does your car, job, or education represent your power and strength? Does your position on the church board or staff represent your spiritual survival? What can you not live without possessing? What have you created as an image to place your trust in? If you trust anything other than God in your life, then you are an idolater. If you worship or submit to anything other than God, you have opened the door for demonic influence in your life.

The second manner of idol worship is creating an image of trust in our mind. "Then he brought me to the door of the gate of the Lord's house which was toward the north; and, behold, there sat women weeping for Tammuz." (Verse 14).

The false god, Tammuz, was an Assyrian fertility god. He was connected to the death of crops in winter and the resurrection to life in spring. The women of Israel cried over his death and mourned the death of their crops. They placed their trust, hope, confidence, and faith in the spring resurrection of this demon god to bring food and sustenance to the community. Instead of trusting the true God of Israel, they resorted to worshiping an imaginary god. They imagined an image of worship and trust.

What do you imagine will pull you through hard times, your dead mother or father? Do you place your trust in an imaginary stock market that will return to life after it had been dead for so long? Do you trust in your denomination, religious traditions, or childhood beliefs about God to get you through life's dark winter? Do you imagine a great career after college that will make you self-confident and financially independent? Are you looking for that perfect man or woman to fulfill all your dreams? The point is that we cannot place trust in things we create in our minds over trust in God for our sustenance.

The third manner in which we can turn to idol worship is to submit and bow down to things that are real. "And he brought me into the inner court of the Lord's house, and, behold, at the door of the temple of the Lord, between the porch and the altar, were about five and twenty men, with their backs toward the temple of the Lord, and their faces toward the east; and they worshipped the sun toward the east." (Verse 16).

In this passage, there are men in the temple of God with their backs toward the Lord and their faces toward the east sun. They are worshipping the sun. The Hebrew word used for worship means to bow down or prostrate oneself. It always connotes paying homage or submitting to a higher authority or being. Once again, when winter destroys all food sources, the spring sun is very important. However, these men were bowing down to the sun and invoking its power to save them. Rather than trust God, these idolaters trusted in the sun, or the spirit of the sun, as a god.

The sun is a real thing, not a humanly created thing, or a thing imagined. What real things do you worship?

What pastor, preacher, teacher, or spiritual leader are you trusting in rather than trusting in God? How about that "Christian" tattoo of a Scripture you placed on your arm? What real church body or building do you submit under rather than submitting to the will of God? Are you trusting in your parent's or spouse's prayers to get you into Heaven? Do you idolize your ministry? Do you bow down to that ministry in submission believing that it will make you a better person in the sight of God?

Idol worship in any form or manner is a very serious thing with God. He is fervently jealous and will punish those who distrust him. And not just for his sake, but for the good of society as well. Violence always follows idolatry. God destroyed the world by a flood because of the great violence on the earth. Violence is a natural outcome of demon worship because demon worship removes a person from obeying God's commandments and taking on his character.

Seriously, consider the three manners of distrusting God through things created, imagined, or real. Pray and ask God to reveal these things in your life, repent, and submit totally to the only God who can save and sustain you in this life and in the one to come. It is no trivial matter.

"Then he said unto me, have thou seen this, O son of man? Is it a light thing to the house of Judah that they commit the abominations, which they commit here? For they have filled the land with violence, and have returned to provoke me to anger: and, lo, they put the branch to their nose. Therefore will I also deal in fury: mine eye shall not spare, neither will I have pity: and though they cry in mine ears with a loud voice, yet will I not hear them." (Verses 17, 18).

Chapter 9: Trash Tradition

"Then came together unto him the Pharisees, and certain of the scribes, which came from Jerusalem. And when they saw some of his disciples eat bread with defiled, that is to say, with unwashed, hands, they found fault. For the Pharisees, and all the Jews, except they wash their hands oft, eat not, holding the tradition of the elders. And when they come from the market, except they wash, they eat not. And many other things there be, which they have received to hold, as the washing of cups, and pots, brass vessels, and of tables." (Mark 7:1-4).

Notice the traditions of man are more important than the truth of God's word. I find it ironic that man would dare to criticize Yeshua, the very word of God made flesh! Things are no different today. God's truth can set us free, but we would rather hold onto false teaching and false doctrine than allow the Holy Spirit to strip us from our traditions and to guide us into all truth. How many times have we heard the following remarks from Christians, "Oh no, we do not believe the gifts of the spirit are for today. Oh no, we do not believe God wants us healed. Oh no, we are too orderly to allow the Holy Spirit to manifest."

"Then the Pharisees and scribes asked him, why walk not thy disciples according to the tradition of the elders, but eat bread with unwashed hands? He answered and said unto them, well hath Isaiah prophesied of you hypocrites, as it is written, this people honors me with their lips, but their heart is far from me. Howbeit in vain do they worship me, teaching for doctrines the commandments of men. For laying aside the commandment of God, ye hold the tradition of men, as the washing of pots and cups: and many other such like things ye do. And he said unto them, full well ye reject the commandment of God, that ye may keep your own tradition." (Verses 5-9).

Yeshua said the religious men neglected the commandments of God so they could keep the tradition of men. This is the definition of religion. It is sin and idolatry. Any rebellion against God is as the sin of witchcraft and stubbornness is as iniquity and idolatry. (1Samuel 15:23).

After the Lord admonished the Pharisees and scribes, the Scriptures teach us that the Lord called the crowd to him again. He began to say to them, "Hearken unto me every one of you, and understand: There is nothing from without a man, that entering into him can defile him: but the things which come out of him, those are they that defile the man. If any man have ears to hear, let him hear."

He continued to teach his disciples and said, "Are ye so without understanding also? Do ye not perceive, that whatsoever thing from without enters into the man, it cannot defile him; because it enters not into his heart, but into the belly, and goes out into the draught, purging all meats? And he said, that which comes out of the man, that defiles the man. For from within, out of the heart of men, proceed evil thoughts, adulteries, fornications, murders, thefts, covetousness, wickedness, deceit, lasciviousness, an evil eye, blasphemy, pride, foolishness: All these evil things come from within, and defile the man."

Yeshua always addresses our need for a savior by exposing our sin. Religion and the traditions of humanity that neglect the commandments of God are sin. This rebellion calls for repentance. We cannot neglect the word of God in order to save tradition. We are warned in Hebrews 2:1-4, "Therefore we ought to give the more earnest heed to the things which we have heard, lest at any time we should let them slip. For if the word spoken by angels was steady, and every transgression and disobedience received a just recompense of reward; how shall we escape, if we neglect so great salvation; which at the first began to be spoken by the Lord, and was confirmed unto us by them that heard him; God also bearing them witness, both with signs and wonders, and with divers miracles, and gifts of the Holy Ghost, according to his own will?" The word, "neglect" is the Greek word "ameleo," which translates "to be careless." We cannot be careless with the word of God.

The Scripture the Lord referenced from Isaiah 29:13 reads, "Because this people draw near with their words and honor me with their lip service but they remove their hearts far from me and their reverence for me consists of tradition learned by rote, therefore behold, I will once again deal marvelously with this people, wondrously marvelous; and the wisdom of their wise men will perish, and the discernment of their discerning men will be concealed."

In John 15:1-6, the Lord teaches his disciples that he is the true vine and the Father is the vinedresser, and they are the branches. He commands his disciples to abide in him so that they could bear fruit. Without the abiding, the branches cannot bear fruit. In verse six, the Lord warns that if anyone does not abide in him, he is thrown away as a branch and dries up; and they gather them, and cast them into the fire and they are burned.

In Matthew 7:15-23, the Lord warns us again. He tells his disciples to beware of the false prophets. They come in sheep's clothing but inwardly are ravenous wolves. The Lord said they would know them by their fruits. The Lord said that not everyone who says to him, "Lord-Lord" will enter the kingdom of heaven, but he who does the will of the Father who is in heaven will enter. Many will say to him on that day, "Lord, did we not prophesy in your name, and in your name cast out demons, and in your name perform many miracles?" And he will declare to them, "I never knew you; depart from Me, you who practice lawlessness." But, according to James 1:27 there is a pure and undefiled religion in the sight of our God and Father, and that is to visit orphans and widows in their distress, and to keep oneself unstained by the world.

Unstained by the world means to love God with all of your heart, strength, and soul. To visit orphans and widows means to love others as yourself. Anything else other than this is ritual and religion, even Christian religion is empty and without merit if it is rooted in the traditions of humankind.

The religion of man that neglects the commandments of God in order to hold onto traditions is a sin and is an idol. It violates the commandment of God to walk in love. But, the pure and undefiled religion that visits orphans and widows in their distress, and to keep oneself unstained by the world is in obedience to the greatest commandment, which is to love God with all our heart, with all our soul, with all our mind, and with all our strength; and to love our neighbor as ourselves. It is time to kill the idol of tradition.

Chapter 10: Flee False Worship

In 1Chronicles chapter 13, we have the Biblical approach for leading others in worship of God. Too many churches allow anyone and everyone on the stage to display their talents and their "look" without taking serious thought if God has chosen those people to lead in worship. Many of today's worship leaders are concerned with creating an "atmosphere" in order for the people to enter into God's presence. They use stage lights, blacked out rooms, multi-media, smoke, cameras, various instrumentations, and everything but the will of God.

Instead of reading God's commands on how to conduct Biblical worship, they attend worship conferences and read worship magazines. This is the blind leading the blind, both falling into a ditch. There is no lasting prophecy in their music, and they succumb to many problems and rebellions within their ministries.

However, there is a Biblical approach to worship that every leader should understand because false worship is idolatry. Many of the churches today have placed an over emphasis on the music and atmosphere while neglecting the foundational word of God. Many have become entertainment centers under the ruse of worship. For many, the worship experience has become an idol that must be slain.

In verses one through four of 1Chronicles, we find King David having good intentions, consulting every leader of Israel about gathering all the people with their priests and Levites to relocate and return the Ark of the Covenant to Jerusalem. Everyone consulted agreed to relocate the Ark because it seemed like the right thing to do. So, King David did some correct things regarding his leadership.

David as leader consulted with his captains both great and small in position, and did not make an independent decision without them. David used two criteria in making the decision to relocate the Ark of the Covenant. The first criterion was, "If it seem good unto you," and the second, "That it be of the Lord our God." Only after consultation, thought and discussion did everyone agree to relocate the Ark of the Covenant.

Then in verses five through eight we read that all of the people were gathered together, placing the Ark on a cart with oxen pulling it. As they moved the Ark, David and all Israel sang, played music, and danced. Nevertheless, this was not the correct way to worship God, and it displeased him.

These are the things done incorrectly. First, there was no consultation with God or his word on "how" to relocate the Ark of the Covenant. Although the "how" was written down in the law that God gave Moses, no one (not even the priests and Levites) told David that there was a correct and incorrect way to worship God. David had consulted with all of his leaders, which was good leadership practice, however he failed to consult with God, which was bad leadership practice.

It was not the "idea" of moving the Ark that was bad. Actually, this idea was a high and noble one containing great intentions and motivation. This idea was not malicious or evil. This idea was pure in its desire to serve God. Yet, it was not the idea that was wrong rather the "how" that was wrong. What was lacking was the "how do we get there from here? How do we do it according to God's principles?"

Many sincere worship leaders and musicians want to lead people to the throne of God, they wish to take them to God's very presence with music and song. This is a noble idea with great intentions. So, the worship leader consults others about his vision, and they agree with his ideas. He then attends a worship conference, and they tell him to darken the room, purchase the best sound system, and use theatrical lighting to set the mood and atmosphere for worship. But, he fails to understand God's proper manner to approach his throne. He fails to grasp the importance of all worship leaders living a holy life before God. So, they worship God in an unscriptural way, which leads to paganism and idolatry.

The second thing David did incorrectly was to allow "all" of Israel to play music before the Lord. God appointed only the Levites to minister before him in music, and so only, the appointed ministers of God should lead in worship today, not anyone or everyone. It matters little how fast a guitarist can play heavy metal riffs, or how beautiful the singers are. Because God was approached incorrectly in worship while moving the Ark, regardless of good intentions, punishment ensued.

"And the anger of the Lord was kindled against Uzza, and he smote him, because he put his hand to the ark: and there he died before God."

The results of inappropriate worship of God are disfavor and punishment. Uzza, although having good intentions, motivation, desire, heart for worship, and a heart to serve God, did so incorrectly. His worship was not according to God's commands. Seeing this unnecessary death, King David becomes angry with God, and then the anger turns into an unhealthy fear of God with a distrust of his character.

Often people with good intentions for worship are not grounded in the "how" of Scripture, and they fail. In failing, they become angry, discouraged, and fearful. Knowing "how" to approach God Biblically is of utmost importance, or else we will be lead astray by false doctrine and practice, bringing into the church the pagan practice of demon worship and new age (occult) philosophies.

Yet, David did not give up on his quest to enter into true worship. David was afraid of God that day, saying, "How shall I bring the ark of God home to me?" Notice that he asks the question, "How" do I do it? God is faithful and answers David. In 1Chronicles 15:2, David discovers God's word and proclaims, "None ought to carry the ark of God but the Levites: for them hath the Lord chosen to carry the ark of God, and to minister unto him for ever."

Here is the key to worship leadership. God "chooses" his worship leaders and participants. Only those "chosen" of God can minister before him. The focus is not the Old Testament priesthood or Levitical law, but on God's "choosing" and "appointing" those to ministry.

We read in verse 13 terrible events happened to Israel when they did not follow God's proper order for worship. "For because ye (The Levites) did it not at the first, the Lord our God made a breach upon us, for that we sought him not after the due order." David then has God's chosen worship leaders, the Levites, chose others among their family to assist them. These worship leaders then appoint their brothers who are skilled in singing and playing music. David as a type of Christ appoints and chooses those who were to lead in worship, and in turn, they appoint their brothers to assist them. The Levites picked people who were skillful at what they did. They were good. Verse 22 tells us, "And Chenaniah, chief of the Levites, was for song: he instructed about the song, because he was skilful."

The results of following God's proper order in worship were God's assistance to the "chosen" worship leaders, giving them success, joy, shouting, singing, and playing of music. Then all of Israel brought the Ark to Jerusalem with praise and shouting. They praised God with "the sound of the horn, with the trumpet, and with cymbals, making music with stringed instruments and harps."

Understand that when God's chosen worship leaders were assisted by God in leading others in worship, then all the people were able to engage in serious worship, sacrifice, and adoration. But, first God's chosen leaders had to lead. Why is it so important to have chosen people lead worship, and in turn, they select and appoint those participants that God chooses?

In chapter 25, the musicians are referred to as prophets. A worship singer or musician should proclaim God's word, his greatness, his majesty, his love, and his return. They "prophecy" in that they exhort the body of Christ, uplift, and lead them into adoration of God. "Moreover David and the captains of the host separated to the service of the sons of Asaph, and of Heman, and of Jeduthun, who should prophesy with harps, with psalteries, and with cymbals." (Verse 1).

The sons of Asaph were under the direction of Asaph, who prophesied according to the order of the king (verse 2), and under the direction of their father Jeduthun who prophesied with a harp to give thanks and to praise the Lord (verse 3) with Heman the king's seer in the words of God, to exalt his horn (verse 5). It should be clear from these passages that worship in the church in vitally important, and it is of exceeding importance to conduct it Biblically. To worship God in an unscriptural way leads to idolatry, pagan practices, new age, and occult performances. No matter what the good intentions are, worship to God has to be godly worship and Scriptural. Let us slay the idols of false worship.

Chapter 11: Slaughter Self

"Trust in the Lord with all your heart; and lean not unto your own understanding. In all thy ways acknowledge him, and he shall direct thy paths." (Proverbs 3:5, 6).

To trust in God is to "attach" to him. Become carefree and "careless" in God and in his word. Do not try to figure things out on your own because you cannot do it. You may want a situation or circumstance to have an outcome, which is generated in your own mind, but God controls the outcomes. He also controls how those outcomes are achieved.

In the Apocryphal book of 1Maccabees, there is an historical account of a battle waged between the warrior Judas Maccabaeus and the Syrian army. The Syrians gathered a large army together to war against Judas Maccabaeus and his small group of warriors. When the small group of warriors saw the vast Syrian army approaching, they said, "How can we, few as we are, fight against so great and so strong a multitude?"

Then Judas replied to his men, "It is easy for many to be hemmed in by few, for in the sight of Heaven there is no difference between saving by many or by few. It is not the size of the army that victory in battle depends, but strength comes from Heaven." (1Maccabees 3:18, 19).

For God, it does not matter what your circumstances are. He delivers regardless of strength or weakness, many or few. The victory is from God. Attempting to understand the issues through human wisdom is futile. Complete trust or attachment to God is the only way to victory.

Judas Maccabaeus not only trusted in God in this battle, but also acknowledged him or "perceived" him in this situation. When we see God in our lives and troubles, he will respond to smooth out the path. This does not mean that work is not involved or that things will be easy, but it means the result will be hammered out and made straight.

Self-confidence is confidence in self, but God confidence is confidence in your standing in him through Christ. Because he is God, all things are possible. One gains confidence in God through respecting, loving, and honoring him. One gains confidence through trust. One gains confidence by fearing him.

In the fear of the Lord confidence grows, "In the fear of the Lord is strong confidence: and his children shall have a place of refuge." (Proverbs 14:26). However, "A wise man fears, and departs from evil: but the fool rages, and is confident." (Proverbs 14:16).

So, with confidence in God, we must commit our life, work, and love to him. Then we can be sure that he will make our plans, intentions, and purposes reliable and firm. The Hebrew word translated "commit" in Proverbs 16:3 means to "roll" oneself onto God or to roll oneself in blood and become dyed red. The picture is of a person covered in blood, dyed red due to their rolling around in the substance. Likewise, we must have that kind of commitment and trust in our Father God. The promise is that he will steady and establish all of our intentions and purposes regarding our works. In other words, we will know what correct choices to make in any situation and circumstance.

"Commit thy works unto the Lord, and thy thoughts shall be established." (Proverbs 16:3). We attach ourselves to God. We roll on him. In all circumstances, we need to trust in his guidance and purpose. In Hebrews 11:30-34, the writer speaks of Israel's heroes of faith. The passage is about some of the bravest, valiant, and faithful men and women in history. Out of weakness, these warriors were made strong, became valiant in battle, and chased away the enemy's armies. They started out weak (in themselves) and became strong (in God, attaching to him). God transformed these ordinary men and women into brave courageous warriors of faith. They became "Ghevers." A Ghever is a Hebrew word referring to a person who is a successful, brave, and valiant warrior or hero. It refers to Israel's past heroes in the prime of their strength.

Proverbs 20:24 uses the Hebrew word Ghever, which is translated "man." But, this word means much more than "man." Ghever is a successful warrior. The passage states that God orders (firms and steadies) the steps of the Ghever (mighty warrior). So how can an ordinary man discern his life's journey?

In other words, the ordinary man who learns to trust in God with all of his heart and does not try to understand things from his own wisdom can become a mighty warrior of faith through the steady guidance and direction from God. The ordinary person begins weak, but ends strong through faith in God. Because of our human weakness, we must rely and trust in God in all of life's situations. This is strength – God's strength.

"Man's goings are of the Lord; how can a man then understand his own way?" (Proverbs 20:24). The passages in Hebrews and Proverbs are stating that God has taken regular ordinary people in weakness and made them strong valiant warriors through trust and faith in him. God is the one directing and guiding their steps. The question is posed, "If God directs the steps of the valiant warrior, why would an ordinary weak person not trusting in God and leaning on their own wisdom think they are able to understand life's journey and purpose?" Attach and roll is the battle cry while slaughtering the idol of self-wisdom and self-confidence.

Chapter 12: Death to Doubt

If we only trust in our senses for the revelation of God in our lives, then we lack true faith in his word. If we state, "I'll believe it when I see it," then we may never believe it or see it. Rather, if we say, "I'll see it when I believe it," then we may see it because we had faith in God. Doubt and unbelief in the word of God can be an idol, which stands in the way of seeing the miraculous in our lives. Often, it is easier to submit and bow down to doubt than it is to submit to faith. However, without faith, we cannot please God. We must put the idol of doubt to death.

In the Gospel of John, there is an account of Yeshua meeting a Samaritan woman, and engaging in a discourse or intellectual discussion with her. She perceived that he was a prophet, and later realized that he was the Messiah or savior of the world. She was so impressed by his words (he knew everything she had ever done) that she went and told many others in her village about Yeshua. Many people in the village believed on Christ based solely on this woman's testimony. She told them that Yeshua knew everything about her, and that he was the savior. She had faith in the logos. She believed (faith, trust, confidence) in our savior because of the words (logos, discourse, communication) with her.

And the other people believed (faith) in Christ based on her testimony. They had not yet seen or talked to Yeshua, yet believed on him based on what the woman said. They had faith in the logos. Without any miracles, signs, or wonders, the Samaritans in that village had faith in Christ and who he was based solely on the words, which were spoken.

And many of the Samaritans of that city believed in him because of the word of the woman who testified, "he told me all that I ever did." And many more believed because of Yeshua' words to them. Then they said to the woman, "Now we believe, not because of thy saying: for we have heard him ourselves, and know that this is indeed the Christ, the savior of the world." (John 4:39-42).

It is so important we as Christ-followers listen and faith in the logos of God. We must believe the word of God as it is revealed to us through the Holy Spirit and Scriptures. We cannot base our faith and walk in Christ on miracles, signs, and wonders. We cannot base our life in God on the spectacular, but on the truth contained in the logos. Yeshua shows this to be true as the account in the Gospel of John continues.

Yeshua leaves the Samaritan village and travels to Galilee and he declares, "A prophet has no honor in his own country." Why did he say this? He said this because he was going into Galilee, his own region. The Galileans had seen him perform miracles in Jerusalem with many witnessing his first miracle of turning water into wine. They "received" him because of the miracles they had witnessed, not because of the logos he spoke.

"Then when he was come into Galilee, the Galileans received him, having seen all the things that he did at

Jerusalem at the feast: for they also went unto the feast." (John 4:45). A nobleman wanted Yeshua to come with him to his house to heal his son, which was near death. Yeshua knowing the Galileans' faith was based on the miracles, which they had observed rather than on his words of truth, said to the nobleman, "You will not believe in me unless you see a miracle." However, surprisingly, the nobleman did not reply to Yeshua' comment, but instead exhibited faith in him. The man simply and urgently restated his request, "Please come with me before my son dies!" Yeshua, knowing this man had faith in him, granted his request, telling him that his son had been healed. And the nobleman believed Christ's word or logos and went home to his son.

The man expressed a clear, articulate, and confident trust in Yeshua' ability to heal his son. He expressed by implication of his acceptance of the yet unseen miracle, his belief that Yeshua was the Messiah sent from God. He "faithed" in Yeshua without first seeing any miracles. His faith was based on Christ's spoken word or logos. Because of this faith in the logos, the man's son was saved from death.

Like the Samaritans before, the nobleman believed (had faith, trust, and confidence) in Yeshua (as the son of God, the savior and Messiah) based on his word (logos, communication, or discourse). They both believed without requiring signs and wonders. They both believed on the spoken word of God through his Son. The account states it clearly.

"So Yeshua came again into Cana of Galilee, where he made the water wine. And there was a certain nobleman, whose son was sick at Capernaum. When he heard that Yeshua was come out of Judaea into Galilee, he went unto him, and besought him that he would come down, and heal his son: for he was at the point of death. Then said Yeshua unto him, except you see signs and wonders, ye will not believe. The nobleman said unto him, Sir, come down ere my child die. Yeshua said unto him, Go thy way; thy son lives. And the man believed the word that Yeshua had spoken unto him, and he went his way." (John 46-50).

As the nobleman was on his way home, his servants met him with the good news that his son was alive and healed. The man questioned the time of the child's recovery and discovered it was the exact same time that Yeshua had spoken the logos word to him. This man's faith resulted in the healing recovery of his son and the salvation of his entire family because they also believed in Christ.

The Scriptures are clear on this concept. Do not base your faith in our savior because you can get self-centered things from the relationship, rather base your faith in him because he is God made flesh and provided redemption for you. Because he is the Son of God and salvation comes only through him. The account in the Gospel of John shows that in both cases of the Samaritans and the nobleman, the miracle occurred after they "faithed" in the words of Christ. Whereas the Galileans "received" him because of his prior miracles they had witnessed, it is unclear whether they continued in their faith and walked with him. It seems that the purer faith comes from listening, hearing, and obeying God's logos word. Let us put the idol of doubt to death, and begin to faith in the word of God.

Chapter 13: Rip Apart Religion

There was a sick man, one who could not walk who lay by a pool of miracles hoping he could be first to get into the water at the right time in order to get healed. As Yeshua was passing by, he saw this man and knew that he had been sick for 38 years. And Yeshua asked this man if he wanted to get well. The obvious answer was "yes," but he could not get into the water fast enough before another received the healing.

Then Yeshua commanded him to do something odd. He said, "Rise, take up your bed and walk." Ok, this has nothing to do with being placed into the pool of miracles for healing. However, the sick man exhibited faith in the logos or in the words of Yeshua before seeing any miracle. He did as he was commanded, and he rose up, picked up his mat, and started to walk. He was immediately healed and made whole. Now, Yeshua commanded this man to do three things. "Yeshua said unto him, rise, take up thy bed, and walk." (John 5:8).

There was a problem with this command. Some would view it as a violation of the law rather than see the wonderful healing, which took place. Yet, Yeshua knew that, and still commanded the man to walk around carrying his sick bed. Why? Yeshua wanted this man to display his redemption publicly. He wanted everyone to know the great power of God. Yeshua could have commanded the man to simply "rise and walk." If the man had risen healed and then walked around, he would not have attracted the attention that he did as when carrying around his bed – on the Sabbath.

The Greek word used for "take up" means to raise, lift, and carry as a burden. It feels the same as the command to "take up your cross and follow me." The cross was an instrument of sin, which Yeshua was nailed to and died. As we Christ-imitators walk and follow Christ, we show our redemption of past burdens, sins, sickness, and despair. We carry our "sin instrument" publicly for all to see. The world needs to see that our cross has our past sins and failures nailed to it, and by the grace of God, we have been saved and healed.

John 5:10-12 discuss the seriousness of the offense of "carrying a burden" on the Sabbath. Why then would Yeshua command this healed man to violate the Sabbath law? The answer is found in Jeremiah 17:21-22. "Thus says the Lord; Take heed to yourselves, and bear no burden on the Sabbath day, nor bring it in by the gates of Jerusalem; Neither carry forth a burden out of your houses on the Sabbath day, neither do ye any work, but hallow ye the Sabbath day, as I commanded your fathers."

The law referred to conducting business on the Sabbath. It referred to carrying burdens of merchandise to sell and trade on the Sabbath. It did not prevent the carrying of non-work related items, like one's coat, staff, or moneybag. The idea here was to separate the Sabbath day to God, and abstain from doing customary business and work. But, the religious leaders in John's account had taken the law to its extreme, placing a yoke of burden on the average person. They missed the fact the healed man had been sick for 38 years, and now was walking! Instead, they focused solely on the violation of their interpretation of the Mosaic Law.

Hosea 2:11 declares the thought of God regarding Israel keeping the ritual of Sabbath while living sinful lives the rest of the week. "I will also cause all her mirth to cease, her feast days, her new moons, and her Sabbaths, and all her solemn feasts."

Also, Amos 8:4-6 reveals what God thinks about people who honor the Sabbath as a ritual, yet continue to cheat and deceive others in business throughout the rest of the week. See, God is not impressed with our attempt at ritual, legalism, and religion. What God desires is obedience to his logos – to his word. "Hear this, O ye that swallow up the needy, even to make the poor of the land to fail, saying, when will the new moon be gone, that we may sell corn? And the Sabbath, that we may set forth wheat, making the ephah small, and the shekel great, and falsifying the balances by deceit? That we may buy the poor for silver, and the needy for a pair of shoes; yea, and sell the refuse of the wheat?"

The people in Amos' day were religious and observed the Sabbath. They also could not wait until it ended so they could cheat others out of their money. God hated this. Likewise, the people in Yeshua' day were observing the Sabbath, but could not recognize the miraculous healing and salvation from God. They could only focus on the violation of their Law. And so, they questioned the healed man about the person who commanded him to carry his bed around on the Sabbath.

He answered them, "He who made me well said to me, 'Take up your bed and walk.'" Then they asked him, "Who is the man who said to you, 'Take up your bed and walk?'" The text does not indicate that the Jewish leaders asked the man about his healing. They were concerned only with finding the man who commanded the cured one to violate the Sabbath law. And for this cause, they sought to kill Yeshua.

The lesson learned from this passage is that every Christ-imitator should "rise, take up their bed, and walk." Every true believer should "pick up their cross and follow Christ." This we all must do regardless of the religious climate of our day, and irrespective of the opinions of those who are under the bondage of idolatrous ritual and legalism. If our savior has redeemed your life, career, or marriage, then we must publicly display that redemption. When we attract the attention of others because of our testimony, then we can point to the miraculous healing of Christ in our lives.

Here is the command of Christ, rise (be healed, saved, redeemed), take up your bed (show the world where you came from and what God had done), and walk (be seen, testify of God's work in your life). Now is the time to rip apart the idols of religion and ritual.

Chapter 14: Annihilate Addictions

Addictions can be tied to almost anything. It is certainly obvious that many addictions, such as, cigarettes, alcohol, caffeine, food, drugs, or sex can be idols standing in the way of true devotion and worship to God. But, what about emotions or certain behaviors, could they be just as addicting? We could write about fear, anger, pride, jealousy, or a myriad of other ungodly characteristics. But, let us examine impatience as an addiction and as an idol.

Although we are learning and becoming better, we have at times been impatient people. Impatience is part of our human character, but not part of God's character. Here lies the problem – if Christ is in us and we are in Christ with all old things dead, and a new creature reborn, then patience must become part of our new character. James, the half-brother of Christ points out the extreme importance of patience as a godly character trait.

"But let patience have her perfect work, that ye may be perfect and entire, wanting nothing." (James 1:4). It is a fact that my God has patience. Patience is one aspect of his character, which translates to one of the fruit of the spirit that all believers must display through their lives. The Prophet Jeremiah called on God's patience, "O Lord, thou knows: remember me, and visit me, and revenge me of my persecutors; take me not away in thy longsuffering: know that for thy sake I have suffered rebuke." (Jeremiah 15:15).

And the Apostle Paul refers to YHWH as the "God of patience" as he admonishes his readers to have the same mind-set of patience as our savior Yeshua. "Now the God of patience and consolation grant you to be likeminded one toward another according to our savior Yeshua." (Romans 15:5).

Yet, character traits of God are not immediately imputed on a person at the moment of salvation, rather they are to be grown into the person through life's situations, troubles, trials, adversities, hopes, joys, promises, and journey. An infant does not have the character of its adult parents, but must grow into an adult through life processes. To be re-born in the spirit is the same. Spiritual infants will develop the character of God as they grow in obedience to his word and direction. It is only God who gives the "right and the power" to become children of God.

The writer of Hebrews commands his readers to examine those who have gone before – who have inherited the promises of God – through faith and patience. The passage demands our imitation of the patient and the faithful. Why? Because that is how we inherit the promises of God. "That ye be not slothful, but followers of them who through faith and patience inherit the promises." (Hebrews 6:12).

So, we take seriously this command not to be sluggish, and we pray this prayer for all of us, "And the Lord direct your hearts into the love of God, and into the patient waiting for Christ." (2Thesolonians 3:5). We also take heed to our Lord's command, "In your patience possess ye your souls." (Luke 21:19).

One day while at work as a manager over police operations, an officer witnessed a terrible car collision, which caused him to request assistance and medical aid to the crash location. I immediately responded. I soon learned that a young 26-year old woman was attempting to turn onto a main thoroughfare from a side street. However, a passenger bus was blocking her complete view of the major highway, thus limiting her sight of approaching traffic.

Impatiently she entered into the roadway regardless of the obstructed view, and collided with a larger vehicle, which was traveling in her direction very fast. The driver of the large truck was a man who was driving with a suspended driver's license. He was not supposed to be on the road that day. He was not hurt, but the young woman instantly died on impact.

After I notified the traffic detectives to respond and take over the collision investigation, I pondered what had just happened. The woman could not wait for the bus to move out of her way. She just had to go even though she could not see approaching traffic and danger. And her impatience with waiting for one or two minutes for the bus to clear the roadway, cost her the young life she had.

The man that struck her was driving with a suspended license. The courts had suspended his license for a reason, for a law violation, but he could not wait either. Impatiently, he just had to drive. His impatience cost the life of a young woman. See, regardless of who was legally at fault, both drivers were impatient. The outcome of this impatience was death and tragedy for everyone involved.

The young woman's car looked like a peeled sardine can. Part of her dead body was dangling outside of her car with signs that she was clearly mangled. Yet, no one, not even the bus driver blocking the victim's view, stopped to assist her. The bus was outfitted with a front camera, which recorded the tragic accident, and yet the bus driver, seeing this horrible accident, pulled away from the curb and drove off without stopping. Why? Impatience. He had a schedule to keep. He had a route to drive. No one on the road that day had the time to stop for this young woman.

God's commands, like putting on his character, are for our own good. If we have the character of Christ and exhibit self-control with love, joy, peace, longsuffering, kindness, goodness, faithfulness, and gentleness – will those traits not benefit us in life? If you have peace, the character of Christ, you will not allow your mind to create that illness in you, that depression, that self-condemnation, that cancer. You will not be slapped on the face by someone you offended, get fired from your job for punching your boss, or end up in jail for disobeying a lawful order if you have self-control. So, if you have patience, you may save the life of your dog, your child, your spouse, or a total stranger on the highway. Let us all examine the obvious and not so obvious addictions in our lives while annihilating the idols that so easily derail us.

Chapter 15: Slay Self Pity

"I have heard of thee by the hearing of the ear: but now mine eye sees thee. Wherefore I abhor myself, and repent in dust and ashes." (Job 42:5, 6).

This is what Job said to God after God revealed himself to Job. After all of the suffering, confusion, anger, and depression, God answered Job with a glimpse of his magnificence. God never explained to Job the reason for his suffering. God never justified himself to man. God only revealed himself, and in the light of this all-powerful God, Job realized that he did not really previously know his God.

Job realized he knew of God only through second hand reports and from hearing about him. He "thought" he knew of God's ways and had placed God in a box governed by human wisdom, knowledge, and principles. When all of this collapsed, Job sought to find God and to be vindicated before him. As God revealed himself in relationship to Job, then he could declare, "But now mine eye sees thee."

During this awful time in Job's life, he had a blatant need for a savior, a vindicator, and a redeemer. He cried for someone in the Heavens to "plead his case" of innocence in his behalf. Job needed an advocate before God. He knew that no man could stand before the all-powerful God to vindicate himself, and so knew he could not save himself. Job actually called on God to plead his case before God. Job knew only God could save man.

In the end, Job could only acknowledge God's power, suddenly seeing his prior relationship with his God lacking in that he never really knew him. Job's repentance had nothing to do with his integrity, because he did nothing wrong, but had everything to do with his relationship to his God. This I why he repented of the words he had spoken.

Job had been a highly moral, ethical, and religious man. He sacrificed to his God, feared his God, and ran away from anything evil. In his human rational thought, these acts of good works would keep calamity and apparent punishment away. Yet, he learned that good works may or may not benefit one on earth, in this temporal life. He learned that God is not governed by principles, but God governs all. God is first. Job saw that good works and religious acts do not save. Only God can save. The relationship with God is primary, with the good works being an outflow of that relationship – not the opposite.

With his physical and spiritual worlds collapsed, he sought to find meaning through finding God. Job never once rejected his God, but complained in bitterness, as all humans do who cannot see the bigger picture and purpose of God's unfathomable greatness. Humanity often forgets God's love coexists with his sovereignty. This is easy to do when all beliefs systems are shattered.

God is not governed by the human principle of justice, but rather he governs principles. We want to see the evil people punished and good people prosper.

Sometimes we do observe this pattern, but not always. We have to know that God's justice will occur, but not necessarily in this lifetime. But, we know that all sinners (those who reject God's salvation) will face eternal death and punishment in the Lake of Fire.

Sometimes, good God-followers suffer. They may even die. We question God and ask why he would allow such good people to suffer badly, and our very foundational beliefs are shaken. Understanding suffering requires an eternal view. God's purposes are eternal and transcend what we see or experience on this temporal earth. As Job never saw the accuser in Heaven getting permission to destroy Job's possessions and health, we do not see the totality of a God that is too great for our understanding. Yet, we know by faith, all things work for good for people who are in God through our savior Yeshua.

Fairness and justice are human concepts created to make sense out of our environment. What we believe is rational behavior or direction is not always the case with God. His actions, purpose, and plans may not necessarily seem rational to us. This is why faith is so important. Without faith, one cannot please God.

Job was a good servant who feared his God. He was morally and ethically blameless, the very qualities that caught God's attention. Yet, he was allowed to suffer through a horrible time for no human rational reason. Job's story does not lend itself to rationality. But, God viewed it in relationship. The relationship and eternal salvation is much more important than temporal "stuff" here on earth, regardless of the pain caused through their loss.

We read in the following verse in James that the end for Job was God's mercy and compassion. It is easy at first glance to think that God's mercy and compassion is related to him restoring Job's possessions and health. But, God's mercy and compassion in the end is not related to Job's "restoration" rather to his "relationship."

If we believe that God showed mercy and compassion on Job in the end by only restoring Job's "stuff," then we can easily cry unfairness because it was God who allowed his stuff to be taken in the first place. The picture is that of a bully who beats and robs a weaker kid, then picks him up, dusts him off, and gives him more money than he originally took. The end does not negate that fact the victim was beaten, humiliated, and robbed. This is not going to create a good relationship.

So, to understand what James wrote about suffering through trials in life, we must view it in "relationship" to God. We must view it through our eternal salvation and purpose glasses. The end for Job was the result of God willingly, mercifully, and compassionately revealing himself to Job.

Prior, Job only heard of God and worshipped him according to what human wisdom believed how he should be worshipped. But in the end, Job saw God and knew God. Job's sufferings were the path used to reveal God in relationship. Centuries later, James would then write about the blessed status of those who can endure,

"Behold, we count them happy which endure. Ye have heard of the patience of Job, and have seen the end of the Lord; that the Lord is very pitiful, and of tender mercy." (James 5:11). We are certainly not telling you that this idol of self-pity is easy to slay, because it is not. In fact, the idol of self-pity and rejection can be so strong that it can derail a Christian from walking in the true spirit of Christ. However, seek God in your circumstances. Try to know the sovereign Lord in all your trials and persecutions while at the same time slaying the idol of self-pity.

Let us finalize this chapter with this call for action. Please, if you are serious about eternal life and living with your Creator God in a kingdom everlasting filled with justice, mercy, and grace, then make an end to all the idols in your life. There are many ways to submit to various forms of idol worship, and we covered only a few ways that are not so common. We selected these uncommon practices of idol worship to get you thinking about other areas in your life that must be controlled and submitted to God through Christ our Lord. This is an ongoing process of sanctification, grace, and holiness. We pray that you take our call for action as serious as any life or death decision - because it is. We pray you have eyes to see the unseen enemies.

Chapter 16: A Unified Christian Language

In this concluding chapter, we wish to give the reader a challenge. Let us all speak a unified "tongue" in our Lord Yeshua our savior. Let us all unite under God's covenant of blessing rather than curse. Allow us to be on "the same page" so to speak. We will have theological differences in matters nonessential to salvation. We will have customary differences in matters of worship and church service that are nonessential to our salvation. However, in matters essential to salvation and pleasing God with our lives, let us unite into one body of Christ.

How do we unite in one godly tongue, speaking the same new language of the Holy Spirit? We believe and we receive. God unites us in his Son. All we need to do is listen to his word, hear it, and obey it. Allow us to give the reader the Scriptural basis for this unity in spiritual language.

Genesis 11:1-9 contains the "antithesis" of Acts 2:1-47. What we mean is that the story of the scattering of the language at the tower of Babel contained in Genesis is the direct opposite of what God did to reunite the spiritual languages on the day of Pentecost contained in the story in the second chapter of Acts. Let us break it all down and you will see with eyes to see when we are finished.

"And the whole earth was of one language, and one speech." (Genesis 11:1). Also, in verse six, "And the Lord said, 'Behold, the people is one, and they have all one language; and this they begin to do: and now nothing will be restrained from them, which they have imagined to do.'" Notice that in Genesis chapter 11, the people were in one accord with one language and purpose, and they could clearly understand each other. In the book of Acts, only the disciples were in one accord on the day of Pentecost, but the rest of the outsiders were still speaking unspiritual Babylonian languages since the scattering from the Tower of Babel. God would reunite them in his language of Christ adding about three thousand to the Ecclesia in one day!

The story of Pentecost contained in the book of Acts chapter two is the exact reversal of the story of "Babel" or Babylon. Babylon always connotes the false mystery religions and paganism of this evil world. So to get out of Babylon is to return to a unified language under Christ. In the gospel of Mark, Yeshua told his disciples "They would speak with new tongues." (Mark 16:18). This predicts the Day of Pentecost when the Ecclesia would come together under a new unified spiritual language of the heart, not with the mouth.

"And when the day of Pentecost was fully come, they were all with one accord in one place." (Acts 2:1). Only the disciples were in one accord and in unity under Christ at this time. The outsiders (the non-believers) were still stuck in the Babylonian matrix since they had been scattered from the Tower of Babel so long ago.

"And there were dwelling at Jerusalem Jews, devout men, out of every nation under heaven." (Acts 2:5).

Also the "scattered" people were, "Parthians, and Medes, and Elamites, and the dwellers in Mesopotamia, and in Judea, and Cappadocia, in Pontus, and Asia, Phrygia, and Pamphylia, in Egypt, and in the parts of Libya about Cyrene, and strangers of Rome, Jews and proselytes, Cretes and Arabians, we do hear them speak in our tongues the wonderful works of God." (Acts 2:9-11).

The people on the outside (Babylonian matrix) remained in multiple languages from various nations. Again, they were the "scattered" from Babel. But, God was going to change that by reuniting them in his tongue. Each one of them heard with their ears their own cultural language praising and glorifying the works of God. This was the beginning of reuniting them into the gospel of our savior.

"Go to, let us go down, and there confound their language, that they may not understand one another's speech." (Genesis 11:7). We see God doing three major things in this passage to stop humanity from building their tower to the heavens for inappropriate and false worship. First, God came down; second, God confounded their language; and third, they could not understand one another's speech. When we look at the second chapter of Acts, we will see God reversing these three mandates for his Ecclesia.

"And suddenly there came a sound from heaven as of a rushing mighty wind, and it filled all the house where they were sitting. And there appeared unto them cloven tongues like as of fire, and it sat upon each of them. And they were all filled with the Holy Ghost, and began to speak with other tongues, as the Spirit gave them utterance." (Acts 2:4). First, God came down as the Holy Spirit just as he came down at Babel. But, instead of mixing the language, he reunited it.

Second, God reunited the languages of the people with a language of the Holy Spirit. "Now when this was noised abroad, the multitude came together, and were confounded, because that every man heard them speak in his own language." (Acts 2:6). The third issue God reversed is their understanding of one another. "And how hear we every man in our own tongue, wherein we were born?" (Acts 2:8).

Remember that God did three things in the Genesis account. First, God came down; second, God confounded their language; and third, they could not understand one another's language. So, to make it clear, the second chapter in the Book of Acts details three things God reversed from the curse of Babel. First, the Holy Spirit came down; second, he reunited the languages; and third, the people could understand one another.

"So the Lord scattered them abroad from thence upon the face of all the earth: and they left off to build the city." (Genesis 11:8). Two things God did to the people as a result of confounding and mixing their language. First, he scattered them over the earth; and second, they quit building the city. In the book of Acts, God reverses this process by gathering his people in one spiritual place, and causing them to start building the city of God within his Ecclesia.

Acts 2:41, "Then they that gladly received his word were baptized: and the same day there were added unto them about three thousand souls." In Genesis, God scattered the people after mixing their language, and now God gathers his people after reuniting them in his holy language of the gospel of Yeshua our savior.

And in Acts 2:42-47 we read, "And they continued steadfastly in the apostles' doctrine and fellowship, and in breaking of bread, and in prayers. And fear came upon every soul: and many wonders and signs were done by the apostles. And all that believed were together, and had all things common, and sold their possessions and goods, and parted them to all men, as every man had need. And they, continuing daily with one accord in the temple, and breaking bread from house to house, did eat their meat with gladness and singleness of heart, praising God, and having favor with all the people. And the Lord added to the church daily such as should be saved."

In the Genesis account, we find the people scattered and ceasing from the building of the city. In Acts, God reversed the curse having his reunited people gathering into the Ecclesia of Yeshua our savior, and building the kingdom of God for the spreading of the gospel.

"Therefore is the name of it called Babel; because the Lord did there confound the language of all the earth: and from thence did the Lord scatter them abroad upon the face of all the earth." (Genesis 11:9). The two reasons the name of Babel was given for the region was one, because the Lord confounded the language of all the earth; and two, because the Lord scattered them upon all the face of the earth. In the book of Acts, we will see that God reversed the name of Babel and gave the name of his Ecclesia, "The Bride of Christ," or "the Church." God reunites his people in one spiritual language and gathers them unto himself.

"And they were all filled with the Holy Ghost, and began to speak with other tongues, as the Spirit gave them utterance." (Acts 2:4). "Then Peter said unto them, 'Repent, and be baptized every one of you in the name of Yeshua our savior for the remission of sins, and ye shall receive the gift of the Holy Ghost.'" (Acts 2:38). In the Genesis story, the name of Babel was given to the region because of confusion and scattering. And now on the day of Pentecost, we read that the name is reversed. God gathered his people and they were baptized in the name of Yeshua our savior for the remission of sins!

No longer should we as the remnant be scattered and confused. We can be reunited in one heavenly spirit language and understanding one another in the spirit of Christ. The name is now called the Ecclesia or the called-out-ones because the Lord reunited the languages in his Christ. The name is Ecclesia because the Lord gathered his people in his Christ. The name is Ecclesia because we have the name of God written in our hearts.

When comparing the antitheses of Genesis chapter eleven with Acts chapter two, we found some other interesting factoids that also add clarity to the understanding of a unified language in Christ.

First, we examined the word "Pentecost" in the book of Acts. The feast of Pentecost was the second of three Jewish feasts, which were yearly celebrated in Jerusalem. Pentecost took place the seventh week after the feast of Passover, and was in recognition of the completed harvest. Notice that the harvest is a time of "gathering" rather than a time of "scattering" as in Babel. Also, note that the "gathering" was to one place, Jerusalem, while the "scattering" of Babel was over the entire earth. Allegorically speaking, we may consider the gathering into Jerusalem as equivalent to the Ecclesia being gathered together to God's New Jerusalem.

The second factoid is found in the word "confound" written in Acts 2:6. The Greek meaning of this word means to co-mingle or to "mix." The verse states that the multitude were confounded or "mixed" because every man heard his language being spoken by the disciples. The "mixing" was the beginning of the "un-mixing" by God. In Genesis, the word confound has in its Hebrew meaning the idea of "mixing" or "mingling." It is used to describe the actions of God as he mixed or confounded the language in Babel. We found it interesting that in both books, Genesis and in Acts, the words meaning to "mix" are found. In Genesis, God "mixed" the language, and in Acts he "un-mixed" the languages.

Genesis 11:2, " . . . They found a plain in the land of Shinar . . ." The Hebrew behind the word translated plain means properly "a split." And the word Shinar means "country of two rivers." We see a third point of interest; there appears to be the idea of a splitting or division in these ancient names. In Acts 2:3, "And there appeared unto them cloven tongues . . ." The word "cloven" is to divide. In Genesis, the land of Babel implied a splitting of the language, whereas in Acts, the split tongues implied a reuniting of the languages.

Finally, we found an interesting concept in the idea of "wind" as it related to both the Tower of Babel and the Holy Spirit in Acts chapter two. In Acts 2:2 we read of a mighty rushing wind filling the house where the disciples were in one accord prior to them being filled and built with the Holy Spirit. We saw that the "wind" in this chapter filled the disciples with the Holy Spirit, which then built the Ecclesia. The wind was positive.

Only in Jeremiah 51:1 have we found a reference to Babylon (not The Tower of Babel) being destroyed by a wind. "Thus saith the Lord; Behold, I will rise up against Babylon, and against them that dwell in the midst of them that rise up against me, a destroying wind."

However, in the ancient book of Jubilees 10:26 it declares, "And the Lord sent a mighty wind against the tower and overthrew it upon the earth." Additionally, the Jewish historian Josephus states, "The Sibyl also makes mention of this tower, and of the confusion of the language, when she says thus: 'When all men were of one language, some of them built a high tower, as if they would thereby ascend up to heaven, but the gods sent storms of wind and overthrew the tower, and gave every one his peculiar language; and for this reason it was that the city was called Babylon.'"

The "wind" filled and built the Ecclesia in the book of Acts while the "wind" destroyed and toppled the Tower of Babylon in the book of Genesis. Clearly, the Tower of Babel where all pagan and false religious worship originated was the antitheses of the day of Pentecost when all true and righteous worship originated through the Holy Spirit.

The unification of the languages under Christ must be discerned spiritually. Romans 7:14, "For we know that the law is spiritual . . ." Also, 1Corinthians 2:13 exhorts, "Which things also we speak, not in the words which man's wisdom teacheth, but which the Holy Ghost teacheth; comparing spiritual things with spiritual. But the natural man receiveth not the things of the spirit of God: For they are foolishness unto him: neither can he know them, because they are spiritually discerned." How do we become spiritually discerning? We become discerning by believing in God's word and keeping his commandments in obedience.

Becoming united into the language of God places God's word in us. Yeshua said to his opponents in John 8:37, "I know that ye are Abraham's seed; but ye seek to kill me, because my word hath no place in you." They did not have God's word or language inside of them, thus they could not understand who Christ was. Yeshua came to reunite in one holy spiritual language his flock, and to gather as one people those who had been scattered so long ago. This gathering into one people is expressed in John 11:49-52, " . . . He prophesied that

Yeshua should die for that nation; and not for that nation only, but that also he should gather together in one the children of God that were scattered abroad."

The Apostle Paul wrote about this unity in Christ in Ephesians 4:4-6, "There is one body, and one spirit, even as ye are called in one hope of your calling. One Lord, one faith, one baptism, one God and Father of all, who is above all, and through all, and in you all." So, how can we be gathered under one spiritual tongue if we have one foot in the kingdom of Christ and one foot in the Babylonian religious system? The Apostle Paul gave us the answer when he wrote in 2Corinthians 6:14-16, "Be ye not unequally yoked together with unbelievers: for what fellowship hath righteousness with unrighteousness? And what communion hath light with darkness? And what concord hath Christ with Belial? Or what part hath he that believeth with an infidel? And what agreement hath the temple of God with idols . . .?"

And what are we to do about attending a post-modern-neo-pagan church steeped in Cultural Christianity? Well, we find the answer in the next verse of the above Scripture. "Wherefore come out from among them, and be ye separate, saith the Lord, touch not the unclean and I will receive you . . ." (2Corinthians 6:17). Let us not forget the words of our Lord Yeshua our savior when he said, "He that hath an ear let him hear what the spirit saith unto the churches. To him that overcometh will I give to eat of the tree of life, which is in the midst of the paradise of God." (Revelation 2:7). And having ears to hear let us hear, and having eyes to see let us see that

Biblical Christianity requires disciples to be like their mentor. "But be ye doers of the word, and not hearers only, deceiving your own selves." (James 1:22).

Ministry Information

KAPOW Radio Show Network

In November 2011, when we published the original eBook edition of "Demons in My Marriage Bed," we had just begun to experiment with an Internet radio show. It is "radio" in the sense that we can conduct live shows, take callers, and run a chat room. It is a "podcast" because all of the shows are archived and can be heard at the listener's convenience.

We needed a name for our show that reflected our passion for teaching others about spiritual warfare and Biblical truths. Linda came up with the name "KAPOW," which stands for Kingdom Against Powers Of Wickedness! A better name did not exist. So, we were off and running and conducted our first show in late October 2011, with one listener, and that was Paul's sister!

However, God kept giving us lessons to teach, words to speak, and the show grew, and is still growing in the grace and power of our Lord Yeshua. Three years later in late 2014, we average 8,000 to 10,000 listeners every 30 days. KAPOW Radio Show has now become a network where we conduct two shows a week and have other like-minded hosts conducting shows for the remaining days. The network provides solid Bible based teaching and discussions throughout the week and listeners can access the content at any time that is convenient for them.

www.kapowradioshow.com

The above website contains all of the information you need to access the shows on the network in addition to containing a radio player on the site. KAPOW Radio Show Network can be downloaded as an iTunes podcast and has its own Apple and Android apps for easy listening. The Network uses both Blog Talk Radio and Spreaker Radio for broadcasting platforms. The KAPOW Radio Show website also contains information about episode schedules with biographies of the network hosts.

The KAPOW Radio Show is produced and sponsored by Fifthook Media, an online digital publisher of eBooks, music, and radio programming. Fifthook Media pays the cost to produce all episodes, and everything is **FREE** to the listener. KAPOW Radio Show does NOT accept monetary donations from anyone. You will never see a "donate" button on the KAPOW or Fifthook Media websites.

www.fifthookmedia.com

In 2010, we wanted to form our own small publishing business so we could write, produce, and publish our own books for distribution to readers. Linda formulated the name from the term, "Fighting For The Heart Of Our King," and thus Fifthook Media was born. Please visit Fifthook Media's website to see our other books about spiritual warfare and Christian living. Additionally, there are many FREE resources on the site as well including free music, free eBooks, and free teaching categorized for your convenience.

Of course, the KAPOW Radio Show can be accessed from this site, and links to the two apps and podcast subscription are there as well. We invite you to explore our site and take advantage of the many resources on there, which will contribute positively to your spiritual growth.

www.facebook.com/fifthookmedia

Join Fifthook Media on face book. This page posts bizarre alternative news in order to stimulate discussion about the evil and perilous times in which we live. Our face book page is dedicated to exposing and warning against the powers of wickedness and evil pervading our planet.

About the Authors

Linda Villanueva earned degrees in Mathematics, Science, and Behavioral Science. She earned a Bachelor of Science Degree in Nutrition and Dietetics from Loma Linda University in California. She has over 25-years in administrative employment with both federal and local governments. Her passion for intercessory prayer and Biblical hermeneutics has enhanced her interest in spiritual warfare. She is the co-author of "Demons in My Marriage Bed: A True Story of Spiritual Warfare," "Eyes to See Unseen Enemies," "Idol'-i-cide: The Killing of Idols," and "Christianity of Blasphemy: A New Gnostic Lie."

Paul Villanueva earned a Bachelor of Arts degree in Biblical Studies and Systematic Theology from Southeastern University in Florida. He received a Master of Arts degree in Negotiation and Conflict Management from California State University Dominguez Hills. He has over 25-years in law enforcement and obtained to the rank of Police Lieutenant. Paul authored "The Wisdom of Death: Six Paths to Understanding Loss and Grief," and "Martial Arts: A Biblical Perspective." He is the co-author of "Demons in My Marriage Bed: A True Story of Spiritual Warfare," "Eyes to See Unseen Enemies," "Idol'-i-cide: The Killing of Idols," and "Christianity of Blasphemy: A New Gnostic Lie."

Books by the Authors

Demons in My Marriage Bed: A True Story of Spiritual Warfare

This book is about saving your marriage from Satan's destruction. It is a true and vivid account about one couple's struggle with witchcraft, spells, curses, and demons all attempting to dismantle their marriage and annihilate them personally.

Paul was involved in an extra-marital affair with a practicing witch. Placed under a demonic love spell, which only the power of God could break, this couple found themselves in a very dark evil world of torment. But, the road back to peace was not an easy one with a very real spiritual-battle taking place for their souls.

Their true story is frightening, as it is the tale of haunted people living a surreal life. However, God trained them to fight with the principles of spiritual warfare, and they teach the reader these Biblical principles, tools, and techniques for battling against the enemy of their marriage.

Most Christian marriages do not reach the dark levels of evil, as the authors' marriage. Yet, they suffer from seldom-recognized demonization in their relationship, which negatively affect them and their families. This book will show you what those tactics are, and how the enemy of your marriage uses them to subtly destroy your marriage.

This is not a book of psychology or counseling. It is a hard-core training manual for building up your marriage to fight the war raging all around you. It trains you and your spouse for a "Martial Marriage." It will teach the both of you to become warriors in Christ.

Christianity of Blasphemy: A New Gnostic Lie

This book is a dire and urgent warning for every Biblical Christian and YHWH fearer still standing. This is a revelation of a cancerous spiritual deception so subtle, ingrained, and invisible, causing many good brothers and sisters to turn to Satan one by one. The current apostasy is paving the way for many to easily receive that horrible death mark from the Beast, as it comes to fruition in a false Christianity.

Because it has rejected the whole truth of Scripture, today's post-Biblical church has turned to an ancient form of Gnosticism. However, the worst is yet to come as this ancient gnosis takes on a new twist from the doctrines of Satan. This new doctrine will merge the Gnostic serpent of enlightenment and experience with a "false Yeshua" already being worshipped.

Unfortunately, many churches, ministries, and universities have already replaced the true Son of YHWH, Yehosua the savior, with a false god, just as ancient Israel replaced YHWH with a Golden Calf. Many in the modern church believe they are worshipping YHWH/Yehosua when in fact they have replaced him with a pseudo-god or antichrist.

Now, in a short time, many will align with the Gnostic "good-god-serpent" of the Garden of Eden boldly declaring that he and their false Christ are one and the same deity. It is coming, and this will be The New Gnostic Christianity of Blasphemy!

Martial Arts: A Biblical Perspective

A 6,000 word well researched mini book on the compatibility between the Martial Arts and Christianity. This work explores the history of ancient fighting arts, the philosophies rooted in the fighting systems, the differences between traditional and non-traditional fighting schools, fitness and heath, Mixed Martial Arts or MMA, the dangers of yogic meditation, and the Biblical viewpoint concerning such practices. It will enlighten your understanding and give you confidence in a decision to practice or not to practice these ancient fighting arts.

This is necessary read for any Christian parent having a child enrolled in any type of fighting art school. It presents a fair and balanced viewpoint supported by documentation and Scriptural references. Many Martial Arts experts were consulted and their views are outlined in a factual manner.

Author, Paul Villanueva holds a second-degree black belt in the Martial Art of Kung Fu San Soo. He has over twenty-five years of law enforcement experience, and was a California state certified instructor in Use of Force techniques for police officers.

He is also a Tactical Communications (Verbal Judo) expert and has appeared on a California state training DVD distributed to every police department in the state. Villanueva earned a Bachelor of Arts degree in Biblical Studies and a Master of Arts degree in Negotiation and Conflict Management.

The Wisdom of Death: Six Paths to Understanding Loss and Grief

The greatest fault found in other grief and loss books is they have not "systemized" the understanding process. Popular works have the information the reader needs so desperately spread throughout their pages or contained in multiple books.

There was a need for a book that plainly and simply "systemized" the journey through death, grief, sorrow, and anger. Needed was a book, which took the wisdom of the ages and applied it to several simple steps or paths.

"The Wisdom of Death: Six Paths to Understanding Loss and Grief" fills that need. It gathers the most important aspects of understanding loss and places them in a six-path system that enables the griever to grasp universal wisdom and truth easily and orderly.

Especially helpful is a "death timeline" where one can approximately determine a loved one's death by observing certain physical and spiritual symptoms. Also, the author discusses methods to responding to others, who are mourning, through a natural empathy. This is called the A.I.M. approach and has assisted many people.

The book contains information in an appendix that discusses financial matters one may face after losing a loved one. This includes a very useful and practical financial checklist. Cons, frauds, and other financial pit-falls are also examined.

Packed with wisdom, practical advice, and a spiritual view, The Wisdom of Death is a necessary book for anyone who has lost a loved one through death. This book was born from first hand experience with the dying process rather than from a cold clinical psychological perspective. The author experienced everything he writes about.

The Wisdom of Death will impart to the reader a better understanding of the dying and grieving process.

###

www.ingramcontent.com/pod-product-compliance
Lightning Source LLC
Chambersburg PA
CBHW070539080426
42453CB00030B/2142